JOANNA FARROW'S
QUICK & EASY
FISH
COOKERY

About the author

Joanna Farrow trained as a Home Economist before spending several years working on women's magazines.

She is currently contributing to a variety of books, magazines and partworks.

With two small children to look after, Joanna fully appreciates the value of quick and easy recipes, whether she is preparing a family meal or entertaining friends.

Joanna loves all aspects of cookery, from imaginative main meals to decorative cakes and pastries. She has written several books including one on microwave fish cookery.

BBC BOOKS QUICK AND EASY COOKERY SERIES

Launched in 1989 by Ken Hom and Sarah Brown, the *Quick and Easy Cookery* series is a culinary winner. Everything about the titles is aimed at quick and easy recipes – the store-cupboard introductions, the ingredients and cooking methods, the menu section at the back of the books. Eight pages of colour photographs are also included to provide a flash of inspiration for the frantic or faint-hearted.

Other titles in the series:

Ken Hom's Quick and Easy Chinese Cookery
Sarah Brown's Quick and Easy Vegetarian Cookery
Clare Connery's Quick and Easy Salads
All at £5.99.

JOANNA FARROW'S
QUICK & EASY
FISH
COOKERY

BBC BOOKS

To my parents for all their help and support

Published by BBC Books,
a division of BBC Enterprises Limited,
Woodlands, 80 Wood Lane, London W12 0TT

First published 1992
© Joanna Farrow 1992
The moral right of the author has been asserted

ISBN 0 563 36324 X

Designed by Peter Bridgewater
Illustrations by Lorraine Harrison
Photographs by James Murphy
Styling by Jane McLish
Home Economist: Allyson Birch

Photoset in Bembo by Redwood Press, Melksham, Wiltshire
Printed and bound in Great Britain by Clays Ltd, St Ives Plc
Colour separations by Technik Ltd
Cover printed by Clays Ltd, St Ives Plc

Front cover photograph: Salmon Wraps with Ginger Butter
Back cover photograph: Grilled Herrings with Spinach and
Pine Nuts

Contents

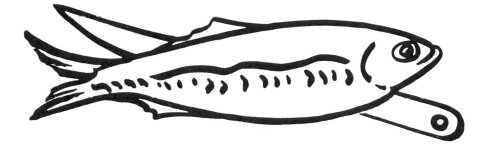

INTRODUCTION

There is a general feeling that preparing fish is complicated and time-consuming. I hope to illustrate this is not so in the following chapters. The recipes require no special equipment or intricate skills, and with the exception of a few seasonal species, the fish are readily available, either from the fishmonger or supermarket. As far as possible the fish I use are bought 'oven ready' to eliminate time-consuming cleaning, filleting and boning.

Like most cookery, the essence of successful fish cookery is that all ingredients used are in prime condition. This does not necessarily mean 'fresh': many supermarkets stock a comprehensive range of frozen fish and while this may not be as desirable as freshly caught fish, it certainly beats produce that has been lying on a wet fish counter for several days, as is unfortunately often the case.

Many of the dishes are based on traditional or classic recipes, adapted to cut preparation and cooking times. I have also borne in mind that the time-conscious cook does not find it easy to shop around, so all the ingredients are readily available from high-street shops. With my love of highly spiced and oriental foods I have tried to reflect the diversity and adaptability of even the commonest fish.

Quick and easy fish dishes can be used not only for family meals, but also for smart dinner parties or casual suppers. Through this book I hope to prove that anybody can both cook and enjoy eating something far more ambitious than the occasional fish grill or fry-up, whatever the occasion.

NOTES ON FISH

BUYING FISH

Take care when buying fish, or you may find yourself cooking something that's well past its best. Whole fish should have a glossy sheen and bright, moist eyes. The flesh of filleted fish should look succulent and smell pleasant, not of seaweed.

Many fishmongers and wet fish counters of supermarkets sell fish that has been previously frozen. This is acceptable as long as you know this when you buy. If you are unhappy with the appearance of the fish, you would be better off buying fish from the freezer cabinet.

Whole prawns must be bought 'whole', with heads intact. Pale, mushy looking prawns should be avoided. If you want whole prawns for the following day, ask the fishmonger for some frozen ones from the back of the shop.

STORING FISH

As far as possible cook fresh fish as soon as possible after buying. Before refrigerating overnight, clean and gut the fish first (if not already done), then cover loosely on a plate. Smoked fish can be stored for up to two days.

PREPARING FISH

Although most of the recipes in this book require fish that is bought ready for cooking, there are occasions when a fish needs scaling, cleaning, scoring or skinning. If you buy from a fishmonger ask him to do the job for you. If not, follow the directions below. All you need is a very sharp knife and a heavy board.

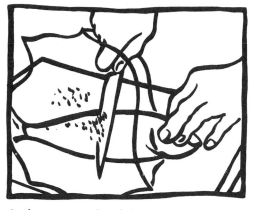

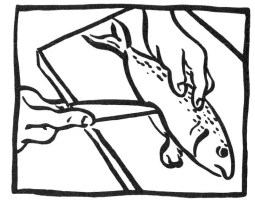

Scaling Lay the fish in a clean plastic bag. Run a knife close to the skin to scrape away the scales. (Keep the fish as far down in the bag as possible, as the scales tend to fly off in all directions!) Turn the fish and repeat on the other side. Rinse the fish well under cold, running water.

Gutting With a sharp knife, slit open the underside of the fish and scrape out the innards. Rinse the fish well under cold, running water.

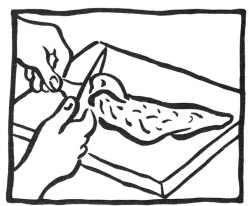

Scoring Scale the fish if necessary then cut several shallow slits down each side of the fish.

Skinning Lay the fillet, skin side down, on the board and hold the tail end with one hand. Starting from the tail end slip a knife between the flesh and skin and gradually 'saw' the flesh away, keeping the knife close to the skin to avoid wastage.

FISH GLOSSARY

BASS

This beautiful firm textured fish should be reserved for special occasions. Baked in foil, a 1–1.5 kg (2–3 lb) specimen makes a stunning centrepiece for a dinner party. Larger fish are sometimes sold in steaks, perfect for grilling.

COD

The success of a dish cooked with cod depends largely on the quality of the fish used. Freshly cooked, the flesh breaks into sweet, succulent flakes, revealing a fine white curd; this is a good indication of freshness. It is a very versatile fish; it comes in steaks or fillets and will endure virtually any cooking method – grilling, frying, baking or battering. Smoked cod lacks the finesse of smoked haddock but makes an acceptable alternative.

COLEY

This is sometimes considered to be a poor relation of cod (due to its coarse flavour and greyish colour), but it is still a worthy buy for everyday pies, fish cakes, soups, stews and any heavily spiced dish.

DOVER SOLE

There is only one way to get your money's worth out of this expensive treat and that is to grill it very lightly and serve with butter and lemon, or one of the butters or sauces mentioned in the chapter on grilling.

GREY MULLET

With a reputation for a coarse texture and 'muddy' flavour, grey mullet might not be a popular choice. However, dressed up with tomatoes, herbs and bacon, and baked in the oven, it can make a thoroughly enjoyable change. Be wary of the coarse scales: these are best removed before cooking.

HADDOCK

For most shoppers, the decision to buy haddock or cod is determined by the price and the cheapest gets the vote. This is not a bad idea as the two are similar in flavour, equally adaptable, and totally interchangeable in any recipe. Traditionally smoked finnan haddock is superior to cheaper forms of smoked haddock and cod to which colouring and flavouring are normally added.

HERRING

Once overfished, and hence unattainable, the herring is now back in abundance, adding variety at the cheaper end of the market. Herrings are highly nutritious and rich in oils. They are best left whole and grilled, fried or baked. Do not discard the roes after cleaning. Add them to extra herring roes from the fishmonger, fry in butter and drizzle with lemon juice for a tempting snack. Herrings are cured in more ways than any other fish. Steeped in a vinegary marinade, they become soused or rollmops. Cold smoked kippers are grilled and served with butter as a traditional breakfast or teatime dish. *Bloaters* are whole herrings, smoked with innards intact to produce a gamey flavour. These can be grilled or mashed to a paste. Hot smoked herrings like *buckling* and *brisling* need no further cooking but a few seconds in the microwave brings out the flavour.

HUSS

Huss is occasionally called flake, rigg, dogfish, or 'rock salmon'; it is instantly recognisable by its pale pink, filleted flesh. Deep fry, or cut from the bone and use in fish cakes and pies.

LEMON SOLE

This is an excellent flat fish that comes between plaice and Dover sole in flavour and price. Grill whole as you would Dover sole or roll the fillets around simple stuffings.

MACKEREL

The baby of the tuna family, mackerel resembles its beautiful cousin in appearance, texture and flavour. Even the smallest is ample for one large appetite so look out for filleted fresh mackerel in supermarket chiller cabinets. Grill or bake mackerel and avoid rich sauces. Instead, opt for tangy citrus and garlic butters. Smoked mackerel, peppered or plain, makes a great lunchtime filler, with lemon or horseradish and crusty bread.

MONKFISH

If you should happen to see a whole monkfish at the fishmonger's do not be put off by its very peculiar appearance. The huge head and blotchy skin, usually discarded before it reaches the slab, hide a delicious white fleshed tail piece with a sweet, firm texture. Sauté in butter or bake in one piece.

PLAICE

Only after sampling Dover or lemon sole does the flavour of plaice suddenly seem inferior. Otherwise it makes a pleasant everyday fish, and is invitingly easy if you simply grill it and serve with a flavoured or plain butter. The same applies to *flounder* and *dab*.

PRAWNS AND SHRIMPS

Nothing can beat buying raw prawns, watching them turn pink as they fry in butter and eating them while still warm. Unfortunately this is an impossibility for most of us and we must make do with the ready-cooked, frozen variety. These are sold whole on the wet fish counter, or peeled and frozen in bags. A deep pink flesh often produces a better flavour. For special occasions buy a few king prawns and use to garnish a cooked prawn dish. Large, ready-peeled vacuum-packed prawns are also widely available. Pink and brown shrimps are sometimes seen at the fishmonger's at a very affordable price. Use them whole for a richly flavoured shellfish bisque.

RED MULLET

A pretty, scaly fish that quickly loses colour once past its best. Distinctively flavoured, small mullet can be wrapped *en papillote* style in greaseproof paper or foil and baked as an interesting starter or main course. Larger mullet can be baked with strong Mediterranean flavours such as garlic, saffron and fennel. Scale them thoroughly before cooking and leave in the livers once gutted.

SALMON

Still one of the most 'regal' of fish, but with the success of salmon farming it is now an affordable luxury. Bake in foil and serve whole as a special-occasion centrepiece or bake, grill or fry the steaks. Salmon tail pieces are usually sold off cheap, perfect for flaking into risottos and pies or some rather special fish cakes.

SARDINES

Fresh sardines are unbeatable if lightly seasoned and grilled, preferably over charcoal. For best results cook on the day you buy them as they deteriorate quickly. Frozen sardines make a reasonable substitute.

SHARK

A really useful fish when you want to cook robust stews or casseroles. The flesh remains chunky, almost meat-like, and can take plenty of strong flavours. Serve grilled as an interesting alternative to other white fish, lavishly basting with flavoured oils or butter to counteract its dryish texture. Select small steaks or let one serve two.

SKATE

One of the best 'everyday' fish that always seems to be available. Poached, fried or grilled, the sweet, succulent strands of flesh fall easily away from the bones. Shredded into chilled salads, it has an appealing shellfish-like flavour.

SNAPPER

A deep-water fish that occasionally makes its way to the fishmonger's slab, and at an affordable price. Under its scaly coat is a pleasantly flavoured, dense-textured fish that is best stuffed and baked.

SPRATS

Small, silvery and herring-like, sprats make a bargain buy for an easy lunch or supper. Remove the heads, but do not bother gutting; shallow-fry with flour or fine oatmeal.

SQUID

Buy these ready-prepared: look for those that are skinned and gutted with the tentacles popped back inside the tubular body. Even better for quick dishes are those that have had everything removed and are ready for slicing into paellas and stews. For a quick snack fry briefly in olive oil until they expand into the familiar rings and add a dash of lemon, sugar and seasoning.

SWORDFISH

A huge fish, abundant in the Mediterranean, and first sampled by most of us on holiday, charcoal grilled. It cooks well this way but also adapts to frying or baking in sauces. Like shark, smother in butter or oil to moisten its dry texture.

TROUT

Trout is best cooked simply, not necessarily fried with almonds, but in plenty of seasoned butter, or baked with bacon and herbs. Prettily coloured, ready-filleted trout can be used as you would cod or haddock, provided accompanying flavours are delicate.

TUNA

Do not be put off by the 'red meat' look of fresh tuna as it lies in great chunks on the fishmonger's slab. Once cooked it resembles canned tuna, but has a much better taste and texture. Baby *bonito* is cooked in the same way.

WHITEBAIT

These tiny, oily fish are usually bought fresh in bags, or from the freezer cabinet, in which case you must thaw and thoroughly dry them before frying. Eat on the same day and deep-fry in seasoned flour.

WHITING

An inferior relative of cod but a welcome alternative if only for a change.

BASIC STORE-CUPBOARD

The majority of the ingredients used in this book are readily available in the shops so there is little need to stock up on a vast array of ingredients that are rarely used, taking up precious larder space. This said, there are many useful oils, pastes and spices which crop up frequently in the recipes and are worth storing if only to reduce shopping loads. This also gives you the opportunity to substitute items should you forget or be unable to buy a particular ingredient.

ANCHOVY ESSENCE

A strong, salty sauce used to cheer up fish pies and sauces. Use it sparingly.

CANNED FISH

If you are prepared to accept that canned fish tastes nothing like the real thing, it does have a useful place in fish cookery, particularly for snacks and quick suppers. The following varieties are particularly worth storage space: *Tuna* now comes in oil, brine or water. The type you choose is a matter of personal preference but find a good quality brand as they vary considerably. Use in snacks, salads or as a store-cupboard substitute for fresh fish in a pie. *Anchovies* have a particularly strong, salty flavour, perfect for rich tomato sauces and salads. They mash into a thick paste which can be blended with butter for topping grilled fish. *Sardines*, in oil or tomato sauce, make an ever-popular snack on toast. They also blend well with cream cheese or thick yoghurt for dips and pâtés.

Smoked and canned *oysters* and *mussels* make tasty pre-dinner appetisers, served on fingers of toast or with a tangy cucumber dip.

GHERKINS AND CAPERS

Although classic additions to tartare mayonnaise (along with parsley), these have a limited use, but can be chopped into hot or cold sauces for a sharper taste. Large, sweet pickled cucumbers make a delicious accompaniment to smoked fish.

HERBS

'Herbs with fish' is as inseparable as 'wine with cheese' and so a good supply is fairly crucial. Unfortunately dried herbs do not fit in with the 'quick and easy' way of cooking as they need plenty of time for their flavours to re-emerge. While this presents a problem for anyone who does not have a good supplier nearby, there are alternatives. Firstly you can buy several packs of fresh herbs on a visit to a large supermarket. Chop them up and freeze them in small cartons or bags. They will darken in colour and be useless for garnish but their flavour will be well preserved. Secondly, keen fish cooks can buy a few basic 'fish' herbs such as tarragon and dill and set them up on the windowsill or allocate a small plot in the garden, cutting and freezing what is left at the end of the season.

Failing these options, stick to fresh parsley which is usually available. Fall back on the dried variety only in recipes such as soups and stews which are given ample cooking.

HORSERADISH

A spoonful of grated horseradish adds bite to a canned fish pâté or dip. Jars of creamed horseradish have a milder flavour so you might need to use extra.

MUSTARD

Grainy mustards are good with fish as they have a more interesting texture and milder flavour than the hot, traditional English ones. Served with smoked fish or add to salad dressings.

OILS

There is an ever-increasing variety of oils now available, each with a different culinary purpose. For pasta and tomato dishes, salad dressings and any recipes with a Mediterranean flavour I prefer to use olive oil which has the finest, richest, nuttiest flavour. Inexpensive, blended vegetable oils are ideal for deep and shallow frying as they can be heated to high temperatures and have little taste. You can use a vegetable oil three to four times for deep frying before it loses its 'frying power'. After use, cool it completely and strain back into a bottle, clearly labelled 'oil for fish'.

PASTA

When you are stuck for an easy supper dish, some cooked spaghetti or pasta shapes, tossed with a tomato sauce and a can of tuna or anchovies, will save the day. Drizzled with olive oil and seasoning, pasta makes a good alternative to rice or potatoes as an accompaniment.

PESTO

This in an Italian sauce made from basil, Parmesan cheese, olive oil and pine nuts. Pungent in flavour, it can be tossed with pasta and canned fish or added to creamy sauces or dips. Refrigerate once the jar has been opened.

SPICES

As a lover of spicy food I have a well stocked spice shelf and frequently incorporate spices into fish cookery. Some of the recipes use whole spices, others ground, although the two are interchangeable. Do not bother buying ground if you have whole in stock and vice versa. The most commonly used in fish cookery are spices for curry such as coriander, cumin, turmeric, chilli and paprika. Nutmeg is good in cheese and herb sauces: buy the seeds whole and grate as required rather than buying ready ground. Another useful spice is saffron, perfect with fish but very expensive. Use it on special occasions.

STOCK

Throughout this book I have tried to avoid using stock cubes as they are a poor substitute for the real thing. Making stock might not be quick but it is certainly easy. Put fresh fish trimmings in a pan with a chopped carrot, onion and a celery stalk and simmer for 30 minutes. Strain through a sieve before using. Fish stock can be stored in the refrigerator for a couple of days or frozen for up to six weeks.

In many of the recipes, wine and water are used when liquid is required, and together with the other ingredients, should give sufficient flavour, but should you find your soup, stew or sauce slightly 'lacking', sprinkle in a little crumbled fish or chicken stock cube.

TOMATO PURÉE

A tube, jar or can of tomato purée makes a good standby for adding colour to, or thickening up, fish soups and stews and tomato sauces, and transforming mayonnaise into a seafood sauce. It often comes ready flavoured with herbs such as basil and marjoram. Look out for 'sun-dried' tomato paste. Sold in jars, often with the addition of oil and herbs, it has a much better flavour than the ordinary purée and is particulary good with Italian and Mediterranean dishes.

VINEGAR

Leaving aside the traditional malt vinegar lavishly sprinkled onto 'fish and chips', white wine vinegar is by far the most useful for fish cookery. A few drops can be used to add zip to a bland sauce or stew, or to take the place of lemon juice in a mayonnaise or hollandaise sauce or any other fish dish in which you have overlooked the lemon or lime. If you make a lot of salad dressings, push several sprigs of fresh herbs into the jar so that the vinegar becomes pleasantly flavoured.

SOUPS AND STARTERS

While you might not contemplate serving a starter for a quick family supper, you may well feel obliged to serve one when entertaining, however casual the occasion. This need not increase your workload enormously as the following pages include some simple pâtés, soups and other more unusual dishes that you need not necessarily confine to the first course. You can even serve as starters small portions of many of the dishes in other chapters. What better than a soup-sized bowl of fish stew on a winter's evening, or some little deep-fried Beignets to whet the appetite?

When we eat out in restaurants we try and choose an interesting contrast between starter and main course and the same applies when planning a fish meal. Follow rich with light, dry with moist, oily with white etc., so that guests have sampled a feast of different colours, flavours and textures in one evening.

However, the most important dishes to choose are those you enjoy. If menu planning gives you a headache it is no longer quick and easy.

SHRIMP BISQUE

S E R V E S
—— 6 ——

PREPARATION TIME
15 minutes
COOKING TIME
35 minutes

*50 g (2 oz) butter
2 large carrots, sliced
1 large onion, peeled and
sliced
450 g (1 lb) whole shrimps
300 ml (10 fl oz) medium
white wine
¼ teaspoon chilli powder
900 ml (1½ pints) water
1 tablespoon cornflour
2 tablespoons tomato purée
85 ml (3 fl oz) double
cream
Salt and freshly ground
black pepper
Extra cream and paprika
to garnish*

The only way to include shrimps in a 'quick and easy' recipe is to use them whole. As delicious as they are, shrimps take simply ages to shell. In this soup they are simmered whole, then blended and strained. Prawns work equally successfully.

Melt the butter in a saucepan; add the vegetables and fry gently for 5 minutes until softened. Rinse the shrimps and add to the pan with the wine, chilli powder and water. Bring to the boil; reduce the heat, cover and simmer for 25 minutes.

Purée in a food processor until smooth. Press through a sieve into the cleaned saucepan. (Most of the pulp will be retained in the sieve but squeeze out as much liquid as possible.) Blend the cornflour with 3 tablespoons of water and add to the pan with the tomato purée and cream. Bring to the boil, stirring, until slightly thickened. Season lightly.

Turn into soup bowls and serve swirled with a little extra cream and a sprinkling of paprika.

FISH CHOWDER

SERVES

—— 4-6 ——

Chowders are fish and potato soup-cum-stews that make a perfectly satisfying main meal, or a warming winter starter if served in smaller portions. To save time the fish fillets are simply simmered on the surface of the soup and then effortlessly flaked into the other ingredients. Here is a good opportunity for using frozen fillets of any white fish you like, such as cod, haddock, coley, whiting or plaice.

Heat the oil in a large saucepan. Add the onion, bacon, potato, bay leaves, curry powder and turmeric and fry for 2 minutes.

Stir in the flour, then stock or water and milk. Bring to the boil and simmer gently for 10 minutes. Stir in the corn.

Lay fish over the soup, cover with a lid and simmer for 2 minutes. Stir the fish into the soup with the cream. Adjust seasoning to taste. Serve hot, sprinkled with chives or spring onion tops.

INGREDIENTS

PREPARATION TIME
8 minutes
COOKING TIME
15 minutes

1 tablespoon vegetable oil
1 large onion, peeled and roughly chopped
100 g (4 oz) smoked streaky bacon, rind removed and sliced
2 medium potatoes, peeled and diced
2 bay leaves
¼ teaspoon curry powder or paste
¼ teaspoon ground turmeric
1 tablespoon plain flour
600 ml (1 pint) stock (see page 16) or water
300 ml (10 fl oz) milk
100 g (4 oz) fresh or canned baby corn, halved (or frozen sweetcorn)
350 g (12 oz) white fish fillets, skinned and boned
3 tablespoons double cream
Salt and freshly ground black pepper
Snipped chives or spring onion tops to garnish

19

SMOKED HADDOCK SOUP

S E R V E S

—— 2-3 ——

A little grapefruit juice adds a welcome 'tang' to this classic, richly flavoured soup which makes a quick lunchtime filler for two or three people. For larger gatherings just double up the quantities. Smoked cod can be substituted for the haddock.

Melt the butter in a saucepan. Add the onion and fry gently for 5 minutes.

Stir in the flour, then stock, milk and fish. Bring to the boil, reduce the heat and simmer gently for 5 minutes.

Stir in the grapefruit juice, cream and seasoning. Reheat very gently but do not boil. Serve hot with granary bread.

INGREDIENTS

PREPARATION TIME
8 minutes
COOKING TIME
12 minutes

25 g (1 oz) butter
1 large onion, peeled and chopped
2 tablespoons plain flour
300 ml (10 fl oz) fish stock (see page 16)
300 ml (10 fl oz) milk
350 g (12 oz) smoked haddock, skinned and boned
Juice of 1 grapefruit
85 ml (3 fl oz) single cream
Salt and freshly ground black pepper

Smoked salmon and watercress soup

Occasionally, delicatessen counters sell smoked salmon 'scraps' – the trimmings from a side of smoked salmon – at a greatly reduced price. Perfectly good in flavour these trimmings are hidden in a creamy, blended soup. Ordinary smoked salmon can also be used, of course, but will work out more expensive.

Discard tough stalks from the watercress. Melt the butter in a saucepan and add the shallots or onion and fry gently for 4 minutes. Stir in the stock.

Purée in a food processor with the smoked salmon until smooth. Add the watercress and blend further until the watercress is finely chopped.

Return to the saucepan and add the wine, cream and seasoning. Heat through gently without boiling. Ladle small portions into bowls and swirl with cream. Garnish with watercress and serve with croûtons.

INGREDIENTS

PREPARATION TIME
10 minutes
COOKING TIME
8 minutes

1 bunch watercress
25 g (1 oz) butter
2 shallots or ⅛ small onion, peeled and finely chopped
600 ml (1 pint) fish stock (see page 16)
225 g (8 oz) smoked salmon
85 ml (3 fl oz) dry white wine
150 ml (5 fl oz) double cream
Salt and freshly ground black pepper
Cream and sprigs of watercress to garnish

SALMON TARTARE

S E R V E S

—— 6 ——

This simple starter will appeal to anyone who enjoys the taste of raw fish, or who needs a gentle introduction to it. Use a reliable fishmonger or supermarket to ensure getting good, fresh salmon, and serve it preferably on the same day.

Roughly chop the salmon then blend in a food processor in short, sharp bursts, scraping fish from the sides of the bowl, until finely chopped but not puréed. (Alternatively finely chop the fish on a board using a sturdy knife.)

Turn the salmon into a bowl and beat in the mayonnaise, herbs and plenty of seasoning.

Scoop the avocado flesh into a bowl and mash lightly with the lemon juice. Stir into the salmon mixture. Spoon onto serving plates and garnish with the herbs. Serve with fingers of toast.

TIP

If you have time, pack the mixture into dampened ramekin dishes then tap them out onto serving plates. This gives a neater presentation.

INGREDIENTS

PREPARATION TIME
20 minutes

450 g (1 lb) fresh salmon
fillets or steaks, skinned
and boned
1 tablespoon mayonnaise
2 tablespoons chopped fresh
dill, tarragon or parsley
2 tablespoons chopped fresh
chives
Salt and freshly ground
black pepper
½ ripe avocado
1 tablespoon lemon juice
A few sprigs of dill,
tarragon or parsley
to garnish

SMOKY TROUT RILLETTES

S E R V E S
—— 4 - 6 ——

The smoky flavour comes from the smoked bacon rather than the fish, giving a rich pâté with an equal balance of flavour. Provided the fish used is fresh, any leftovers can be potted and left in the fridge for up to a week, making a delicious snack for spreading on hot buttered toast. Smoked trout can be used equally well.

Melt the butter in a frying pan. Add the onion and bacon and fry gently for 5 minutes. Add the trout to the pan with the wine. Bring to the boil and simmer for 2 minutes until the fish is cooked through.

Blend in a food processor to a smooth paste. Leave to cool, then chill until required. Serve on a bed of lettuce with fingers of toast.

INGREDIENTS

PREPARATION TIME
10 minutes
COOKING TIME
7 minutes

25 g (1 oz) butter
1 small onion, peeled and roughly chopped
100 g (4 oz) smoked streaky bacon, chopped
225 g (8 oz) trout fillet, skinned and boned
85 ml (3 fl oz) dry white wine

PASTA SHELLS WITH GARLICKY PRAWN SAUCE

SERVES
—— 4 ——

For lovers of pasta, garlic and seafood this starter is sheer indulgence. Double up on quantities for an even more indulgent main course.

Cook the pasta in plenty of boiling salted water until just tender; drain.

Heat the oil in a small saucepan. Add the garlic and fry for 1 minute. Add the wine, tomato purée, prawns (which can still be frozen) and paprika. Blend in a food processor with the cream until smooth.

Remove heads and shells from the king prawns, leaving tails intact. Return the pasta to a large pan with the prawn sauce, king prawns, chopped tomatoes and seasoning. Heat through gently without boiling, and serve garnished with herbs.

INGREDIENTS

PREPARATION TIME
7 minutes
COOKING TIME
12 minutes

*150 g (5 oz) pasta shells or
other pasta shapes
3 tablespoons olive oil
2 cloves garlic, peeled and
crushed
4 tablespoons dry white
wine
1 tablespoon tomato purée
100 g (4 oz) frozen peeled
prawns
¼ teaspoon paprika
150 ml (5 fl oz) double
cream
8 king prawns
4 tomatoes, de-seeded and
diced
Salt and freshly ground
black pepper
Several sprigs fresh basil,
coriander or parsley*

SOURED CREAM AND PRAWN GRATINS

SERVES
— 4 —

If you serve this starter in pretty scallop-shaped heatproof dishes, you might convince your guests that this recipe took much longer to prepare than it actually did. Otherwise use small ramekins and surround them with whole prawns and plenty of greenery.

Use poached and flaked white fish instead of prawns if you want to economise.

Pre-heat the oven to gas mark 5, 190°C (375°F). Combine the cream, parsley, prawns and seasoning in a bowl. Spoon into four small dishes.

Melt the butter and mix with the breadcrumbs. Spoon over the dishes. Place on a baking sheet and bake for 10–15 minutes until turning crisp and golden. Serve hot, garnished with whole prawns and parsley.

INGREDIENTS

PREPARATION TIME
10 minutes
COOKING TIME
10–15 minutes

150 ml (5 fl oz) soured cream
1 tablespoon finely chopped fresh parsley
225 g (8 oz) peeled prawns
Salt and freshly ground black pepper
40 g (1½ oz) butter
25 g (1 oz) breadcrumbs
A few whole prawns and leaf parsley to garnish

BLINI WITH SMOKED SALMON

SERVES
— 4 —

Traditional *blini* are small, yeast-raised Russian pancakes often made with buckwheat flour. This cheat's version is basically no more than a dropped scone but tastes just as good as a *blini*. Allow three per serving and arrange them prettily on plates with a little smoked salmon, spoonful of soured cream and, if available, lumpfish roe, for a thoroughly enjoyable starter. Once you have cooked the required number of *blini*, chill any remaining batter and make fresh blini for serving with cheese or cold meats.

Sift the flour with a pinch of salt into a bowl. Make a well in the centre. Break the egg into the well and add a little of the milk. Whisk the egg and milk, gradually incorporating the flour to a smooth batter. Stir in the remaining milk and the chives.

Heat a little oil in a frying pan. Add one dessertspoonful of the batter for each *blini* and fry in batches for 1 minute until golden on the underside. Flip over and cook the other sides. Slide out of the pan and keep warm.

Arrange *blini*, smoked salmon, soured cream, lumpfish roe and herbs on serving plates.

INGREDIENTS

PREPARATION TIME
12 minutes
COOKING TIME
5 minutes

---

100 g (4 oz) self-raising flour
1 egg
150 ml (5 fl oz) milk
2 tablespoons chopped fresh chives or spring onion tops
A little oil for frying
100 g (4 oz) smoked salmon
4 tablespoons soured cream
4 teaspoons red or black lumpfish roe
A few sprigs of parsley, dill or tarragon to garnish

POTTED SEAFOOD

SERVES
—— 4-6 ——

The combination of prawns, salmon and skate, encased in butter, makes an equally delicious, yet not quite as rich a variation on traditional potted prawns. It is one of those easy starters which you can make well ahead (even the day before) and leave in the fridge, knowing that the flavour can only improve with keeping. Serve with daintily cut fingers of brown bread or toast.

Place the salmon and skate in a pan with the milk. Cover with a tight-fitting lid and cook over a very gentle heat for 3 minutes. Turn the fish and cook for a further 3 minutes. Drain the fish and leave to cool.

Lightly flake the salmon, discarding the skin and any bones. Roughly shred the skate, discarding the cartilage. Mix with the prawns and divide among 4–6 individual ramekin dishes. (Alternatively place in one large dish.) Pack the fish down lightly.

Melt the butter in a small saucepan. Add the nutmeg and a little seasoning. Spoon over the fish and chill for at least 30 minutes. Serve garnished with whole prawns and watercress.

INGREDIENTS

PREPARATION TIME
10 minutes
COOKING TIME
7 minutes

175 g (6 oz) salmon tail piece
1 small skate wing (about 225–300g/8–10 oz)
1 tablespoon milk
225 g (8 oz) peeled prawns
90 g (3½ oz) butter
A generous pinch of grated nutmeg
Salt and freshly ground black pepper
A few whole prawns and sprigs of watercress to garnish

TROUT CEVICHE WITH PICKLED CUCUMBER

S E R V E S
— 4 —

By marinating fish in lemon juice for several hours overnight or while you are at work, the fibres are softened and it takes on a cooked appearance and flavour. After marinating, the fish can be arranged prettily on serving plates with a spoonful of sweet pickled cucumber, which can also be made well in advance.

Cut the trout fillets diagonally into 1 cm ($\frac{1}{2}$ in) wide strips. Place in a dish with the bay leaves and peppercorns. Mix together the lemon juice and sugar and spoon over the fish. Cover loosely and chill for at least 6 hours or overnight, turning the fish once at the most convenient time.

To make the pickled cucumber, simmer the onion in vinegar, sugar and mustard, covered with a lid, for about 5 minutes. Add the cucumber and cook for a further 2 minutes. Blend the cornflour with a little water and add to the pan, stirring until thickened. Leave to cool then season lightly and transfer to a bowl.

Drain the trout from the liquid and arrange on serving plates. Add a spoonful of the pickle and garnish with parsley and bay leaves.

TIP

If you want to serve straight pieces of trout, make sure you arrange the strips uniformly in the dish before you add the marinade. As the strips marinate they will 'set' in the position in which they are laid.

INGREDIENTS

PREPARATION TIME
15 minutes (plus marinating time)
COOKING TIME
8 minutes

---

450 g (1 lb) trout fillet, skinned and boned
2 bay leaves
2 teaspoons black peppercorns
5 tablespoons lemon juice
2 tablespoons caster sugar

PICKLED CUCUMBER
½ small onion, peeled and finely chopped
50 ml (2 fl oz) white wine vinegar
25 g (1 oz) caster sugar
1 tablespoon grainy mustard
¼ small cucumber, thinly sliced
½ teaspoon cornflour
Salt and freshly ground black pepper
A few sprigs of leaf parsley and bay leaves to garnish

SMOKED MACKEREL AND HORSERADISH PÂTÉ

S E R V E S
—— 4-6 ——

Without doubt, this is one of the easiest starters. Spoon onto plates with a salad garnish or pack into little ramekin dishes.

———

Blend the fish in a food processor with the melted butter, lemon or lime rind and horseradish until pale and light, scraping up any unblended fish from the sides of the bowl.

Season to taste and add extra horseradish if liked. Turn onto plates or into dishes and garnish with lemon or lime. Serve with warm toast.

INGREDIENTS

PREPARATION TIME
5 minutes

225 g (8 oz) smoked mackerel fillet, skinned and flaked
50 g (2 oz) butter
Grated rind of 1 lemon or lime
1 tablespoon creamed horseradish
Salt and freshly ground black pepper
Lemon or lime wedges to garnish

LAYERED PLAICE AND VEGETABLE MOUSSE

SERVES

— 6 —

INGREDIENTS

PREPARATION TIME
15 minutes
COOKING TIME
35–40 minutes

*450 g (1 lb) broccoli,
roughly chopped
4 eggs
300 ml (10 fl oz) double
cream
A generous pinch of freshly
grated nutmeg
Salt and freshly ground
black pepper
2 large plaice fillets,
skinned*

SAUCE
*4 tablespoons mayonnaise
Grated rind and juice of ½
lemon
2 tablespoons single cream*

This is not the time-consuming, 'set' sort of mousse but rather a quick vegetable purée, layered with the fish and baked until just firm. I have used broccoli for the purée which contrasts perfectly in colour and flavour, but you could substitute spinach, asparagus or peas. Lemon sole or trout may be used instead of plaice.

Pre-heat the oven to gas mark 4, 180°C (350°F). Lightly butter individual ramekin dishes. Cook the broccoli in a little boiling salted water for about 5 minutes. Thoroughly drain and purée in a food processor with the eggs, double cream, nutmeg and a little seasoning until smooth. Spoon half the purée into the dishes.

Cut the fish into six even-sized pieces. Lay over the purée, then cover with the remaining purée. Place in a roasting tin. Pour 1 cm (½ in) depth of boiling water around the dishes and cover loosely with foil. Bake for 30–35 minutes until just firm.

For the sauce, beat together the mayonnaise, lemon rind and juice and cream and serve in a small jug.

SARDINES
IN TOMATO SAUCE

SERVES
— 4 —

The rich flavour of fresh sardines quickly mingles with the tomatoes to give an appetising starter that needs little extra flavouring. It is worth making double quantities as any leftovers are equally good served cold with a bowl of olives and some warmed olive bread.

Fry the onion in the oil until slightly softened, then add the tomatoes, tomato purée, sugar, thyme and a little seasoning and cook for 5 minutes or until pulpy. Bury the sardines in the sauce and cook for a further 5 minutes. Serve warm.

INGREDIENTS

PREPARATION TIME
10 minutes
COOKING TIME
10 minutes

1 large onion, peeled and
finely chopped
2 tablespoons olive oil
1 × 400 g (14 oz) can
chopped tomatoes
2 tablespoons tomato purée
2 teaspoons caster sugar
1 teaspoon chopped fresh or
¼ teaspoon dried thyme
Salt and freshly ground
black pepper
450 g (1 lb) fresh or frozen
sardines, de-headed
and cleaned

Special seafood cocktail

SERVES

—— 6 ——

PREPARATION TIME
20 minutes
COOKING TIME
10–13 minutes

SESAME PASTRIES
1 × 200 g (7 oz) packet
puff pastry
1 egg, beaten
Sesame seeds

350 g (12 oz) monkfish,
boned and chopped into
small chunks
10 g (½ oz) butter
Salt and freshly ground
black pepper
225 g (8 oz) peeled
prawns
Curly endive, radicchio
and cherry tomatoes for
garnish

SAUCE
4 tablespoons mayonnaise
2 teaspoons grainy mustard
1 teaspoon lemon juice
1 teaspoon tomato purée
4 tablespoons double cream
A good pinch of caster
sugar
2 tablespoons chopped fresh
parsley, tarragon, dill or
watercress

No chapter on fish starters would be complete without some variation on the prawn cocktail. This one combines prawns and monkfish in a creamy herb mayonnaise. If you prefer, stick to prawns and increase the quantity but buy some whole king prawns and even a scattering of shrimps to garnish for a good effect.

As a more interesting alternative to buttered brown bread I have included some sesame pastries which can be cut into triangles or fun shapes using small cutters. These can be made in advance and re-heated just before serving. Alternatively serve some crusty bread instead.

First make the sesame pastries. Pre-heat the oven to gas mark 7, 220°C (425°F). Roll the pastry out thinly and cut out triangles or shapes using biscuit cutters. Brush with beaten egg and sprinkle with sesame seeds. Bake for 8–10 minutes until risen and golden. Transfer to a wire rack to cool.

Fry the monkfish in the butter for 2–3 minutes. Season lightly and leave to cool.

To make the sauce, beat together the mayonnaise, mustard, lemon juice, tomato purée, cream, sugar, herbs and seasoning.

Arrange the monkfish, prawns and salad garnish on serving plates. Spoon over the sauce and serve with the pastries.

PASTA SHELLS WITH GARLICKY PRAWN SAUCE (PAGE 24)

Smoked haddock 'soufflés' with lemon dressing

SERVES
— 6 —

These dainty fish starters are quite soufflé-like in texture but don't involve the traditional whisking or sauce-making. For this recipe the preparation can be done well in advance but, as with the risen version, the soufflés need to be served as soon as they are cooked.

Pre-heat the oven to gas mark 4, 180°C (350°F).

For the dressing, cut away the rind from the lemons then cut between the membranes to release the segments. Place the segments in a blender or food processor. With the machine running, gradually add the oil, a little at a time, until the mixture thickens. Stir in the sugar and transfer to a small saucepan.

Lightly butter the base and sides of six individual ramekin dishes. Cut the haddock into small chunks and place in the blender with the eggs. Blend to a paste, scraping the mixture around sides of bowl into the centre. Beat in the cream and pepper and divide the mixture among the ramekin dishes. Stand the dishes in a roasting tin and add boiling water to the tin to a depth of 1 cm (½in). Cover with foil and bake in the oven for 20 minutes until the centres feel just firm.

Towards the end of the cooking time gently heat the dressing and arrange the frisée and olives on serving plates. Loosen the soufflés from their moulds by running a knife around the edges then turn them out onto the plates. Pour over the dressing and serve immediately.

INGREDIENTS

PREPARATION TIME
20 minutes
COOKING TIME
20 minutes

DRESSING
2 lemons
6 tablespoons olive oil
1 tablespoon caster sugar

350 g (12 oz) smoked haddock, skinned and boned
3 eggs
75 ml (3 fl oz) soured cream
Freshly ground black pepper
½ small frisée
12 black olives

INDONESIAN HOTPOT (PAGE 41)

SPEEDY STEWS

For the more conventional eater, the idea of tackling unidentified pieces of fish, swimming around in a bowl of liquid, might be a little offputting. However, fish stew makes one of the most enjoyable dishes, as the fish and accompanying ingredients have time to mingle into a delicious pot full of flavour. Serve with some crusty bread for dipping in the juices, some wine and a salad, for a thoroughly enjoyable and utterly complete meal.

Usually made with two or more types of fish, stews can be a little expensive to make. For this reason I have included a variety, both simple and elaborate. The Easy Fish Stew on page 38 uses everyday white fish and prawns, combined with potato in a creamy sauce. This is a good one to try first.

I have also included a recipe for Rouille, a hot garlicky paste, stirred into stews to add even more flavour.

MONKFISH AND BACON STEW

SERVES

—— 4-6 ——

Like any fish stew, the ingredients for this dish can be mixed and matched to suit your mood, or what you have in the fridge. You can swap lean gammon for the bacon, fennel for the celery, tomatoes for the pepper, and sliced onions for the shallots, but you must keep the monkfish, wine and cream as the combination is delicious.

Discard the cartilage from the monkfish and cut the fillet into chunks. Heat the oil in a large pan. Add the shallots and bacon, cover with a lid and cook gently for 5 minutes until the shallots have softened slightly. Add the celery, then blend in the flour. Gradually stir in the wine and stock or water.

When all the liquid has been blended in, bring the mixture to the boil, reduce the heat and add the monkfish, mustard and red pepper. Cover with a lid and cook over a low heat for 15 minutes. Finally, stir in the cream and seasoning and heat through gently. Serve sprinkled with tarragon or parsley.

INGREDIENTS

PREPARATION TIME
12 minutes
COOKING TIME
25 minutes

---

700 g (1¹/₂ lb) monkfish tail
2 tablespoons olive oil
12 shallots, peeled and left whole
110 g (4 oz) streaky bacon, rinded and sliced
4 sticks celery, sliced
2 tablespoons plain flour
300 ml (10 fl oz) dry white wine
300 ml (10 fl oz) stock (see page 16) or water
1 tablespoon grainy mustard
1 red pepper, de-seeded and diced
150 ml (5 fl oz) double cream
Salt and freshly ground black pepper
Sprigs of tarragon or parsley to garnish

EASY FISH STEW

SERVES
—— 4 ——

The flavours of these basic ingredients blend beautifully to make a good stew. Peel the whole prawns beforehand or serve fingerbowls and let your guests peel their own.

Melt the butter in a large saucepan and fry the leeks and garlic for 2 minutes.

Add the stock and bring to the boil. Add the potatoes and cook for 10 minutes or until just tender.

Cut the fish into large chunks and add to the saucepan together with the prawns and cream and cook for 3 minutes. Season lightly and serve with croûtons or bowls of rice.

INGREDIENTS

PREPARATION TIME
12 minutes
COOKING TIME
15 minutes

25 g (1 oz) butter
2 large leeks, sliced
2 cloves garlic, peeled and crushed
600 ml (1 pint) fish stock (see page 16)
450 g (1 lb) potatoes, peeled and cubed
675 g (1½ lb) cod or haddock fillet, skinned and boned
110 g (4 oz) peeled prawns
8 large whole prawns
4 tablespoons double cream
Salt and freshly ground black pepper

ITALIAN FISH STEW

S E R V E S

—— 4·6 ——

A though I suggest using white fish such as cod, coley, huss, haddock or plaice in this stew, you can be really adventurous as anything goes. It is cooked rapidly so that the juices reduce to a deliciously garlicky 'gravy'; the result is a lucky dip for keen fish eaters, but not for those who are cautious with bones.

———

Cut the white fish into small steaks. Cut the heads and tails from the mullet or snapper, then halve or quarter each fish. Discard the cartilage from the monkfish and cut each fillet into three. Slice the squid if using.

Mix the tomato purée with the herbs, sugar and wine.

Heat the oil and fry the onions and garlic for 5 minutes. Drain. In a large saucepan, layer up the fish, onions and tomatoes, seasoning lightly as you layer until they are all finished. Sprinkle with the olives and pour the wine mixture over the top.

Cover and cook rapidly for 5 minutes. Remove the lid and cook quickly for 15–20 minutes until the juices have thickened slightly. Serve garnished with the herbs.

TIP

Serve plenty of bread for mopping up the juices. Warmed Ciabatta bread is particularly good.

INGREDIENTS

PREPARATION TIME
20 minutes
COOKING TIME
25–30 minutes

450 g (1 lb) white fish fillet, skinned and boned
450 g (1 lb) red mullet or snapper, scaled and gutted
450 g (1 lb) monkfish
225 g (8 oz) prepared squid (optional)
2 tablespoons tomato purée
2 tablespoons chopped fresh basil, oregano or parsley, or 1 teaspoon dried
1 teaspoon caster sugar
150 ml (5 fl oz) dry white wine
4 tablespoons olive oil
3 large onions, peeled and sliced
3 cloves garlic, peeled and crushed
450 g (1 lb) tomatoes, quartered
Salt and freshly ground black pepper
12 black olives
Extra herbs for garnish

ROUILLE

A dash of Rouille paste can be used to add zip to many white fish stews and soups. It keeps well in the refrigerator for up to a week, after which any leftovers are good for adding spice to a meat or chicken casserole.

Blend the pepper, garlic, chilli and oil in a food processor until smooth. Add the breadcrumbs and blend until paler in colour. Transfer to a small dish and store, tightly covered, in the refrigerator.

INGREDIENTS

PREPARATION TIME
3 minutes

1 red pepper, de-seeded and chopped
4 cloves garlic, peeled and chopped
1 fresh chilli, chopped, or 1 teaspoon chilli seasoning
4 tablespoons olive oil
25 g (1 oz) breadcrumbs

INDONESIAN HOTPOT

SERVES
—— 4-6 ——

This rich, chunky broth, oozing with noodles and nuts, falls somewhere between a soup and a warming one-pot meal. It is based on a recipe that starts with a blended and fried nut paste, to which the stock, fish etc., is added. As a shortcut I have used peanut butter which makes a convenient thickener yet produces the same full flavour.

———

Heat the oil in a large pan or wok. Add the garlic, spring onions and ginger and fry for 1 minute. Add the peanut butter, soy sauce, chilli powder, lime, sugar and stock and bring to the boil. Simmer for 5 minutes.

Add the fish, nuts, noodles, peas and red pepper. Cover and simmer for a further 10 minutes.

TIP

The chilli and ginger give quite a fiery flavour. Cut down on both if you do not like the heat.

INGREDIENTS

PREPARATION TIME
15 minutes
COOKING TIME
16 minutes

2 tablespoons vegetable oil
4 cloves garlic, peeled and crushed
1 bunch spring onions, white parts only, roughly chopped
2.5 cm (1 in) piece fresh root ginger, peeled and grated
3 tablespoons peanut butter
2 tablespoons dark soy sauce
½ teaspoon chilli powder
grated rind of 1 lime
1 teaspoon light brown sugar
1.5 litres (2⅔ pints) chicken or fish stock (see page 16)
700 g (1½ lb) cod, haddock or coley fillet, skinned, boned and cut into chunks
50 g (2 oz) cashew or peanuts
75 g (3 oz) thread egg noodles
75 g (3 oz) peas
1 red pepper, de-seeded and sliced

SHELLFISH STEW

S E R V E S

—— 4-5 ——

PREPARATION TIME
12 minutes
COOKING TIME
18 minutes

*2 tablespoons olive oil
1 large onion, peeled and
chopped
2 celery stalks, sliced
1 small fennel, trimmed
and sliced
2 carrots, sliced
2 tablespoons plain flour
300 ml (10 fl oz) stock or
water (see page 16)
150 ml (5 fl oz) vermouth
3 tomatoes, chopped
225 g (8 oz) crabmeat
225 g (8 oz) peeled
prawns
4 tablespoons double cream
Salt and freshly ground
black pepper
A few sprigs of leaf parsley
to garnish*

However gifted you are at extracting the meat from a whole crab, the task is by no means quick and easy. Fortunately, fishmongers or the wet fish counters in supermarkets stock ready-dressed crab. This has usually been frozen and is not good for eating on its own, but combined with many other flavours it makes a perfectly acceptable base for a rich shellfish stew. If you cannot obtain crabmeat, substitute crabsticks. Roughly chopped and stirred into the stew, you should get away with it!

Heat the oil in a large saucepan. Add the onion, celery, fennel and carrots. Fry for 3 minutes. Add the flour, then blend in the stock or water and vermouth. Bring just to the boil, reduce the heat and simmer for 10 minutes.

Stir in the tomatoes, crabmeat and prawns and cook very gently for 5 minutes. Add the cream and season to taste. Serve garnished with parsley.

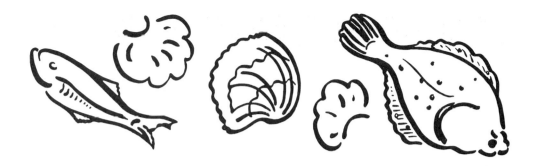

OVEN BAKES

One of the advantages of oven-baked fish recipes is that you can make the dish, pop it in the oven, set the timer and leave it to take care of itself. Included in this chapter are some cheesy potato pies, smarter 'pastry' pies, stuffed fish and some interesting wrapped fish dishes. Baking wrapped fish, whether in greaseproof paper or foil, is one of the simplest, yet most impressive techniques. It might be as simple as cod steaks with two or three other ingredients sealed in foil cases, such as Fish and Feta Parcels (p. 53), or the more extravagant Whole Baked Fish in Foil (p. 63). If you find the thought of serving a whole baked salmon quite daunting, this recipe makes a highly rewarding introduction. It does away with fish kettles, which are expensive, and poaching stocks, and gives very good results. A variation on this style of cooking is the *en papillote* method. Whole fish or fish steaks are wrapped in greaseproof paper, again with plenty of herbs, seasonings etc., and baked in a hot oven. When cooked, the fish is served still in the parcels, and each diner is treated to a promising waft of the enclosed fish as they pierce open the paper.

COD AND COCKLE PIE

S E R V E S

—— 4 - 6 ——

I have included two pies for the simple reason that the variations on this theme are endless. Although both the recipes are quite different in flavour they share an easy one-stage cheese sauce in which flour, butter, milk and cheese are blended, then heated to thicken – far quicker than traditional methods.

PREPARATION TIME
20 minutes
COOKING TIME
55–65 minutes

700 g (1½ lb) potatoes, peeled and cut into chunks
350 g (12 oz) smoked cod
350 ml (12 fl oz) milk
40 g (1½ oz) butter
75 g (3 oz) mature Cheddar cheese, roughly cubed
25 g (1 oz) plain flour
1 large leek, sliced
100 g (4 oz) cockles in brine, drained
Salt and freshly ground black pepper

Pre-heat the oven to gas mark 5, 190°C (375°F).

Boil the potatoes in salted water for 15–20 minutes until tender, then drain.

Place the cod in a saucepan with a dash of the milk. Cover and simmer gently for 5 minutes. Drain, reserving the liquid. Flake the fish, discarding the skin and any bones.

Blend the fish cooking juices with the remaining milk, 25 g (1 oz) of the butter, the cheese and the flour in a food processor. Transfer to a saucepan and cook for 2 minutes, stirring continuously.

Melt the remaining butter in a frying pan. Add the leek and fry for 3 minutes, stirring.

Roughly slice the potatoes and place half in a large pie dish. Layer up the leeks, cod and cockles. Arrange remaining potatoes over the filling.

Season the sauce if necessary and pour over the potatoes. Bake for 30–35 minutes until surface is bubbling and golden. Serve hot with a side salad.

FISH PIE WITH BLUE CHEESE AND CELERIAC

SERVES

—— 4-6 ——

Pre-heat the oven to gas mark 5, 190°C (375°F). Then cook the potatoes and celeriac in boiling salted water for 15–20 minutes until tender. Drain and mash well.

Place the fish in a saucepan with a little of the milk. Cover and simmer gently for 5 minutes. Drain, reserving the liquid. Roughly flake the fish, discarding the skin and any bones.

Blend the fish cooking juices, remaining milk, butter, flour and cheese in a food processor until smooth. Transfer to a saucepan and cook, stirring until thickened.

Place half the potato mixture in a large, shallow pie dish. Layer up with the broad beans and the fish. Season the sauce if necessary and pour half over the filling. Spoon the remaining potato over the pie and cover with the remaining sauce. Bake for 30–35 minutes until the surface is turning golden. Serve hot with a salad.

INGREDIENTS

PREPARATION TIME
15 minutes
COOKING TIME
50–60 minutes

350 g (12 oz) potatoes, peeled and cut into chunks
350 g (12 oz) celeriac, cut into chunks
450 g (1 lb) cod, haddock, coley or huss
350 ml (12 fl oz) milk
25 g (1 oz) butter
25 g (1 oz) plain flour
100 g (4 oz) Danish Blue or Stilton cheese, crumbled
100 g (4 oz) broad beans
Salt and freshly ground black pepper

ROAST MONKFISH

S E R V E S

—— 4 - 5 ——

INGREDIENTS

PREPARATION TIME
15 minutes
COOKING TIME
21–26 minutes

1 large monkfish tail, about
900 g (2 lb)
1 clove garlic, peeled and
sliced
3 tablespoons olive oil
1 large onion, peeled and
chopped
3 cloves garlic, peeled and
crushed
A small handful rosemary
sprigs, snipped
Salt and freshly ground
black pepper

Although rather too expensive for everyday eating, a generous sized monkfish tail can be simply, yet interestingly cooked for a supper party main course. Tie it up and smother it with garlic and onions well in advance, ready for last-minute cooking.

Do not be disappointed by the slightly 'shrunken' appearance after baking – the delicious flavour of both fish and juices makes up for it. For a perfect accompaniment try the Pepper Coulis on page 75.

———

Pre-heat the oven to gas mark 5, 190°C (375°F).

Remove any of the loose skin from the monkfish and cut away the central bone to leave two long fillets. Lay the fillets side by side with a thick end against a thin. Using cotton or fine string tie the fillets together at 2.5 cm (1 in) intervals. Tuck the slices of garlic between the fillets.

Heat the oil in a frying pan and cook the fillets for 1 minute, turning once, to seal. Transfer to a shallow oven-proof dish.

Add the onions and crushed garlic to the pan and fry gently for 5 minutes until softened. Add the rosemary to the onions with a little seasoning. Spoon over and around the monkfish.

Bake for 15–20 minutes until cooked. Insert a knife between the fillets to check if the fish is cooked. If the flesh in the middle is opaque, then it is ready. Snip and pull away the string before serving.

SPICED FISH PILAU

SERVES

— 6 —

This recipe is very similar to a spicy Indian Biryani but takes half the time to prepare. I have retained the whole spices, but these can be replaced with a teaspoon of curry powder or paste if you need an even quicker version. The tiny black seeds of cardamom pods are normally picked out from the pods before cooking, but they can be left intact – it saves time and adds authenticity.

Pre-heat the oven to gas mark 4, 180°C (350°F).

Bring a pan of salted water to the boil. Add the rice and the whole eggs and cook for 8 minutes until the rice is almost tender; drain. Shell the eggs and roughly slice.

Roughly crush the cardamom pods, cumin and coriander. Cut the fish into bite-sized pieces.

Heat the oil in a frying pan. Add the onions, garlic, ginger, crushed seeds, flaked almonds, turmeric, cloves and cinnamon and fry gently for 5 minutes. Combine in a large ovenproof serving dish with the rice, eggs, fish, sultanas, prawns and plenty of seasoning.

Cover and bake for 40 minutes. Serve sprinkled with the coriander.

INGREDIENTS

PREPARATION TIME
20 minutes
COOKING TIME
58 minutes

450 g (1 lb) long-grain or
basmati rice
4 eggs (in shells)
1 tablespoon cardamom
pods
2 teaspoons cumin seeds
2 teaspoons coriander seeds
4 tablespoons vegetable oil
3 medium onions, peeled
and sliced
3 cloves garlic, peeled and
crushed
5 cm (2 in) piece fresh root
ginger, peeled and chopped
50 g (2 oz) flaked almonds
$\frac{1}{2}$ teaspoon ground turmeric
8 cloves
1 cinnamon stick, halved
450 g (1 lb) cod, coley or
haddock, skinned and
boned
50 g (2 oz) sultanas
100 g (4 oz) whole prawns
Salt and freshly ground
black pepper
2 tablespoons chopped fresh
coriander

SEAFOOD VOL-AU-VENT

S E R V E S
— 4 —

INGREDIENTS

PREPARATION TIME
30 minutes
COOKING TIME
43 minutes

*2 × 400 g (13 oz) packets
of puff pastry
1 egg, beaten for glaze
3 tablespoons olive oil
1 large onion, peeled and
chopped
4 cloves garlic, peeled and
crushed
2 celery stalks, sliced
1 × 700 g (1½ lb) can
tomatoes
1 teaspoon caster sugar
2 teaspoons mixed dried
herbs
450 g (1 lb) cod or haddock
fillet, skinned and boned
100 g (4 oz) frozen
prawns, thawed and
drained
Salt and freshly ground
black pepper
6–8 king prawns*

This recipe is a sure winner when you want to impress guests with your pastry work. The secret is to roll the pastry thickly so that it rises dramatically during cooking, laden full of luxurious filling.

This dish can also be served as a starter for six to eight people.

Pre-heat the oven to gas mark 7, 220°C (425°F).

Lightly grease a baking sheet. Roll out both the sheets of pastry until just 24 cm (9½ in) in diameter. Place one sheet on top of the other, then using an upturned bowl or plate 24 cm (9¼ in) in diameter, cut out a round. Transfer to the baking sheet. Cut out the centre of the upper sheet, leaving a 2 cm (¾ in) rim, and remove. Brush the top of the pastry only with beaten egg and bake for 20 minutes until well risen.

Heat the oil in a saucepan and fry the onion, garlic and celery for 3 minutes. Add the tomatoes, sugar and herbs and cook rapidly for 5 minutes or until pulpy. Cut the fish into chunks and stir in with the prawns and seasoning.

Spoon into the pastry case and garnish with the whole prawns. Cover with a piece of foil and bake for 15 minutes. Serve warm with a leafy salad.

TANDOORIED FISH

SERVES

— 4 —

This recipe does not have the bright orange colouring or the 'pasty' coating of a classic tandoori dish. Instead the spices and yoghurt coat the fish thickly – a perfect guise for coley. Haddock or cod can be substituted, for a more expensive dish.

Pre-heat the oven to gas mark 6, 200°C (400°F).

Mix together all the ingredients except the fish.

Cut the fillet into four portions. Lightly oil a large shallow ovenproof dish. Lay the fish in the dish and lightly cover with the yoghurt mixture.

Bake for 25–30 minutes until the sauce is beginning to brown. Serve hot with a mixed salad and rice.

INGREDIENTS

PREPARATION TIME
15 minutes
COOKING TIME
25–30 minutes

5 cm (2 in) piece fresh root ginger, peeled and grated
2 cloves garlic, peeled and crushed
3 tablespoons natural yoghurt
2 tablespoons vegetable oil
1 tablespoon tomato purée
¼ teaspoon ground turmeric
2 teaspoons ground cumin
2 teaspoons ground coriander
¼ teaspoon chilli powder
1 tablespoon garam masala
700 g (1½ lb) coley fillet, skinned and boned

TROUT
WRAPPED IN BACON

SERVES
— 2 —

Trout and bacon make a perfect partnership and are used here in a classic, yet very simple dish. Substitute fresh herbs such as rosemary, fennel, dill or chervil for the tarragon and use ready filleted trout if you do not have time to fiddle with bones. The richness of the fish needs a light refreshing accompaniment such as a cucumber salad, or, when in season, minted marrow.

INGREDIENTS

PREPARATION TIME
5 minutes
COOKING TIME
25 minutes

2 small trout, cleaned and gutted
Several sprigs tarragon
1 tablespoon snipped fresh chives or spring onion tops
4 rashers smoked back bacon, rind removed

Pre-heat the oven to gas mark 4, 180°C (350°F).

Score the flesh of each trout several times down each side. Tuck the tarragon into the body cavities.

Sprinkle the trout with the chives and wrap each in two rashers of bacon. Lay them in a shallow ovenproof dish and bake for 25 minutes until turning crisp and golden. Cover with foil during cooking if overbrowning.

BAKED MACKEREL WITH BROWN ALE

S E R V E S
— 4 —

Ready-filleted mackerel, now available at many supermarkets, will suit all those who find a whole mackerel far too rich to tackle. Finished in a brown ale sauce, it develops an almost 'meat in gravy'-like taste, perfect for mid-week winter evenings with plenty of mashed potatoes and green beans, or even cabbage!

Pre-heat the oven to gas mark 4, 180°C (350°F).

Lay the mackerel in a shallow ovenproof dish.

Melt the butter in a small saucepan. Add the onion and fry gently for 2 minutes. Add the ale and mustard and bring to the boil. Season lightly and pour over the fish.

Cover with a lid or foil and bake in the oven for 20 minutes. Serve hot.

INGREDIENTS

PREPARATION TIME
5 minutes
COOKING TIME
22 minutes

4 large mackerel fillets
10 g (½ oz) butter
1 onion, peeled and thinly sliced
225 ml (8 fl oz) brown ale
1 teaspoon grainy mustard
Salt and freshly ground black pepper

CHEESY TROUT LASAGNE

S E R V E S

—— 4 ——

PREPARATION TIME
20 minutes
COOKING TIME
42 minutes

*350 g (12 oz) trout fillets
400 ml (15 fl oz) milk
40 g (1½ oz) butter
40 g (1½ oz) plain flour
A generous pinch of freshly
grated nutmeg
A small handful of parsley
175 g (6 oz) Gruyère or
Cheddar cheese
4 eggs, hard-boiled
150 ml (5 fl oz) single
cream
Salt and freshly ground
black pepper
150 g (5 oz) green lasagne
sheets*

Virtually any white fish can be substituted in this recipe, although the pink trout makes a pretty contrast against the pale green pasta. To save time use the lasagne sheets that need no pre-boiling. For the sauce adopt the blender method used for the pies on pages 44–5, throwing in the parsley and cheese to save on chopping and grating.

Pre-heat the oven to gas mark 5, 190°C (375°F).

Place the trout in a large pan with a little of the milk. Cover and cook for 5 minutes. Drain the fish, reserving juices. Flake the fish, discarding the skin and any bones.

Blend the butter, flour, reserved juices and milk lightly in a food processor. Add the nutmeg and parsley. Roughly cut up 100 g (4 oz) of the cheese and add to blender. Process until the parsley is finely chopped.

Place the sauce in a pan and bring to the boil, stirring until thickened. Slice the eggs into the sauce, stir in the cream and add the fish and seasoning.

Place alternate layers of sauce and pasta sheets in a shallow ovenproof dish, finishing with a layer of sauce. Grate the remaining cheese over the surface.

Cover with foil and bake for 15 minutes. Remove the foil and bake for a further 20 minutes until the surface is turning golden. Serve hot with a mixed salad.

FISH AND FETA PARCELS

S E R V E S
—— 4 ——

Crumpled foil makes very convenient containers for baked fish dishes, keeping flavour and juices neatly concealed in each portion, and saving on washing up. The filling can be as simple as you choose: a piece of fish, dot of butter, slice of tomato and sprinkling of herbs and seasoning is all you need for an irresistibly easy meal. This recipe combines cod or salmon, feta and mint.

Pre-heat the oven to gas mark 6, 200°C (400°F).

Tear off four sheets of foil, each about 25 cm (10 in) square. Place a cod or salmon steak in the centre of each.

Sprinkle the feta, mint and pepper over the steaks. Place 2 prawns with each steak and season lightly. Spoon 2 teaspoonfuls of olive oil over each.

Bring the edges of the foil up over the filling and crumple together. Place on the oven shelf and bake for 25 minutes. Serve hot with new potatoes and a green vegetable.

INGREDIENTS

PREPARATION TIME
5 minutes
COOKING TIME
25 minutes

4 cod or salmon steaks
100 g (4 oz) feta cheese, diced
A small handful of fresh mint, roughly chopped
½ small red pepper, de-seeded and diced
8 whole prawns
Salt and freshly ground black pepper
3 tablespoons olive oil

BRAISED MULLET WITH BEANS

SERVES
— 4 —

PREPARATION TIME
8 minutes
COOKING TIME
32 minutes

2 tablespoons olive oil
1 large onion, peeled and chopped
2 cloves garlic, peeled and crushed
1 × 400 g (14 oz) can haricot beans, drained
1 × 225 g (8 oz) can red kidney beans, drained
150 ml (5 fl oz) red wine
2 teaspoons chopped fresh or ½ teaspoon dried rosemary
Salt and freshly ground black pepper
4 small red mullet, scaled and gutted

The firm texture and meaty taste of red mullet deserves a robust style of cooking. Here it is braised on a bed of beans which soften during cooking to flavour the rich, garlicky sauce – perfect for mopping up with crusty bread.

I've used haricot and red kidney beans, but substitute butter, flageolet, black-eyed, mixed beans or anything else you can find. Snapper or grey mullet can be used instead of red mullet.

Pre-heat the oven to gas mark 4, 180°C (350°F).

Heat the oil in a large flameproof casserole dish. Add the onion and garlic and fry for 2 minutes. Stir in the beans, wine, rosemary and seasoning.

Bring to the boil. Lay the fish over the surface and cover with a lid. Bake for 30 minutes and serve hot with bread or boiled potatoes.

TIP

If you don't have a flameproof casserole dish, use a saucepan to make the bed of beans and transfer it to a shallow oven-proof serving dish. Alternatively use a roasting tin, covered with foil.

SHARK
WITH ALMOND SAUCE

SERVES
— 4 —

Creamy almond sauces, so popular in Middle Eastern and Indian cuisine, can easily be adapted to fish cookery. Reduce the spices, enrich with cream and you have a delicious sauce that perfectly complements meaty fish like shark and swordfish.

Pre-heat the oven to gas mark 4, 180°C (350°F).

Heat the oil and fry the onion, ginger, bay leaves, cinnamon and turmeric for 3 minutes. Add the stock, ground almonds and fish and bring to the boil.

Transfer to a casserole dish. Cover with a lid and bake for 35 minutes.

Add the tomatoes to the dish. Season to taste and return to the oven for a further 5 minutes. Stir in the cream, sprinkle with the flaked almonds and serve garnished with bay leaves.

TIP

The almond sauce will thicken quickly if not served immediately. If necessary stir in a little extra stock or milk to give a thinner consistency.

INGREDIENTS

PREPARATION TIME
10 minutes
COOKING TIME
43 minutes

3 tablespoons olive oil
1 large onion, peeled and chopped
2.5 cm (1 in) piece fresh root ginger, peeled and grated
2 bay leaves
1 cinnamon stick, halved
A good pinch of ground turmeric
450 ml (15 fl oz) fish stock (see page 16)
60 g (2½ oz) ground almonds
900 g (2 lb) shark steaks, skinned and boned
100 g (4 oz) cherry tomatoes, quartered
Salt and freshly ground black pepper
3 tablespoons double cream
2 tablespoons flaked almonds, toasted
Fresh bay leaves for garnish

SALMON WRAPS
WITH GINGER BUTTER

SERVES
— 4 —

Simple to prepare yet impressive enough for the smartest dinner party, this dish relies on precise cooking; if over-done, it will quickly spoil. Rather than unwrap each beautifully prepared parcel to check if the fish is cooked, loosen a corner of one and prod the tip of a skewer into the salmon steak – the flesh should be moist and only just 'opaque' in the centre. To complete the meal, serve some minted new potatoes and a crisply cooked vegetable such as broccoli or mangetout peas. Red mullet can be substituted for salmon.

INGREDIENTS

PREPARATION TIME
15 minutes
COOKING TIME
25 minutes

25 g (1 oz) butter
4 salmon steaks
2.5 cm (1 in) piece fresh root ginger, peeled and grated
Grated rind of 1 small orange, plus 4 strips of pared rind
2 teaspoons chopped fresh parsley
Salt and freshly ground black pepper
A few sprigs of flat-leaf parsley to garnish

Pre-heat the oven to gas mark 5, 190°C (375°F).

Cut out four rounds of greaseproof paper, about 25 cm (10 in) in diameter. Smear the centres with half of the butter. Lay a salmon steak to one side of each round of paper so that the other half can be brought up over the salmon.

Sprinkle the ginger over the salmon with the orange rind and parsley. Season lightly and dot with the remaining butter.

Bring the greaseproof paper up over the salmon to en-close it completely, then fold and roll the edges of the paper together to seal. Transfer to a baking sheet and bake for 25 minutes. Serve hot garnished with parsley.

If you're really out to impress, enclose two cleaned, closed and undamaged mussels in each parcel before sealing. During cooking they will open out to make an attractive garnish.

Smoked haddock and pear pastries

SERVES
— 4 —

This combination of ingredients may seem a little unusual, but the pears provide plenty of moisture and perfectly complement the smoky flavour of the fish. Apples or pineapple would work equally well if you can only find rock-hard pears. Smoked cod can be used for haddock.

Pre-heat the oven to gas mark 7, 220°C (425°F).

Lightly grease a baking sheet. Cut the fish into four even-sized pieces. Roll out the puff pastry thinly, and cut out a 41 × 25 cm (16 × 10 in) rectangle. Cut the rectangle into eight sections. Space four of the pieces on the baking sheet. Lay a piece of fish in the centre of each. Spread with the mustard, and place one pear quarter and a knob of butter on each. Season lightly.

Brush the edges of the pastry with beaten egg. Lightly score the remaining pastry sections through the centres, then lay them over the filling and press the edges firmly down onto the pastry bases to seal.

Brush with beaten egg to glaze and bake for about 20 minutes until the pastry is risen and golden. Serve warm with a leafy salad.

INGREDIENTS

PREPARATION TIME
15 minutes
COOKING TIME
20 minutes

350 g (12 oz) smoked haddock, skinned and boned
1 × 375 g (13 oz) packet of puff pastry
2 teaspoons grainy mustard
1 ripe pear, peeled, quartered and cored
25 g (1 oz) butter
Salt and freshly ground black pepper
Beaten egg to glaze

COD AND SAFFRON PIE

SERVES

—— 4-6 ——

INGREDIENTS

PREPARATION TIME
20 minutes
COOKING TIME
28–33 minutes

350 g (12 oz) potatoes,
peeled and 'chipped'
1 teaspoon (1 sachet)
saffron strands
2 × 375 g (13 oz) packets
of puff pastry
450 g (1 lb) cod fillet,
skinned, boned and roughly
sliced
1 large onion, peeled and
chopped
1 green or red pepper,
de-seeded and sliced
50 g (2 oz) butter, softened
3 cloves garlic, peeled and
crushed
Beaten egg to glaze

Another puff pastry pie, this time an impressively large one that combines fish with vegetables and oozes a garlicky saffron butter. A good recipe for making ahead, this pie will sit happily in the fridge overnight before cooking. Any other white fish, trout or salmon can be used in place of the cod.

Pre-heat the oven to gas mark 7, 220°C (425°F).

Lightly grease a large baking sheet. Cook the potatoes in boiling salted water for 3 minutes to soften; drain.

Mix the saffron with 1 tablespoon of boiling water and leave to stand.

Roll out one sheet of pastry to a rectangle measuring at least 30.5 × 20.5 cm (12 × 8 in). Transfer to the baking sheet. Scatter the fish over the pastry base to within 2.5 cm (1 in) of the edges. Scatter the potatoes, onion and pepper over the fish. Pour the saffron and water through a sieve and drizzle the saffron juices over the pie.

Beat together the butter, garlic and saffron strands and dot over the pie. Brush the edges of the pastry base with beaten egg. Roll out the remaining pastry until large enough to cover the pie. Position over the pie and press the edges down onto the base to seal. Trim off any excess pastry.

Brush the pie with beaten egg to glaze. Bake for 25–30 minutes until risen and golden, covering with foil if the pie starts to overbrown.

TIP

If there's time decorate the pie with leaves made from the pastry trimmings. Alternatively score the pastry diagonally with the tip of a sharp knife.

QUICK FILO 'QUICHE'

S E R V E S
—— 4 - 5 ——

As the name suggests this is an easy version of a quiche, using frozen filo pastry as a quicker alternative to making your own shortcrust. Provided you keep any pastry you're not working with covered to prevent drying out, filo is easy to manage and left-overs can be re-frozen.

Pre-heat the oven to gas mark 5, 190°C (375°F).

Cut the fish into chunks. Heat 1 tablespoon of the oil in a frying pan and fry the onion for 3 minutes.

Place the spinach in a sieve and press out excess liquid. Mix the cheese with the spinach, onion and fish.

Beat together the eggs, cream, nutmeg and plenty of seasoning.

Use one pastry sheet to line the base and sides of a 20.5–23 cm (8–9 in) tart tin letting excess pastry overhang edges. Brush with a little of the remaining oil. Add three more layers of pastry, brushing each with oil.

Spoon the fish mixture into the centre, then pour over the cream mixture. Bring the excess pastry up over the filling. Crumple up the remaining two sheets of pastry over the top of the quiche and brush with any remaining oil. Bake for 35 minutes until the pastry is golden.

INGREDIENTS

PREPARATION TIME
20 minutes
COOKING TIME
38 minutes

350 g (12 oz) cod or haddock fillet, skinned and boned
2 tablespoons vegetable oil
1 onion, peeled and chopped
1 × 450 g (1 lb) packet of frozen leaf spinach, thawed
100 g (4 oz) feta cheese, diced
2 eggs
150 ml (5 fl oz) single cream
A generous pinch of grated nutmeg
Salt and freshly ground black pepper
6 sheets filo pastry

PLAICE WITH CHORIZO STUFFING

S E R V E S
— 4 —

PREPARATION TIME
10 minutes
COOKING TIME
25 minutes

150 g (5 oz) chorizo or
kabanos sausages
50 g (2 oz) breadcrumbs
2 tablespoons tomato purée
or ketchup
Salt and freshly ground
black pepper
8 plaice fillets, skinned
1 large beefsteak tomato cut
in wedges, or 4 plum
tomatoes, sliced or 225 g (8
oz) cherry tomatoes
15 g ($\frac{1}{2}$ oz) butter

Rich Mediterranean-style sausages make the easiest, yet tastiest stuffing, coming complete with garlic and spice. All you need do is blend them. These stuffed and rolled plaice fillets are baked on a bed of tomatoes. Avoid the ordinary, mildly flavoured tomatoes and go for cherry, beefsteak or, best of all, fresh plum tomatoes which make a delicious buy in the autumn. Lemon sole can be substituted for plaice.

———

Pre-heat the oven to gas mark 5, 190°C (375°F).

Roughly cut up the sausages and blend in a food processor with the breadcrumbs, tomato purée or ketchup and seasoning. (Alternatively mash the sausages then beat in the remaining stuffing ingredients.)

Spread the fish with the stuffing. Roll up and place in an ovenproof dish with the loose ends tucked underneath. Arrange the tomatoes around the fish and season lightly.

Dot the fish with butter and cover the dish with foil. Bake for 25 minutes. Serve hot with spaghetti.

GREY MULLET
STUFFED WITH BACON

SERVES
—— 4 ——

The flavour of grey mullet is not very highly rated, but it does deserve a mention, particularly if finished with a meaty stuffing of herbs and bacon. Serve with oven chips and grilled tomatoes for a good, everyday meal. Snapper makes a good alternative to grey mullet which is not regularly available.

———

Pre-heat the oven to gas mark 5, 190°C (375°F).

Lightly butter a shallow ovenproof dish.

Reserve two rashers of bacon and finely chop the remainder. Mix the onions with the bacon, breadcrumbs, herbs, lemon rind and juice and seasoning. Pack into the fish cavity.

Lay the mullet in the dish and wrap the reserved bacon around it. Dot with butter and bake for about 30 minutes or until cooked through to the bone. Serve hot.

TIP

To speed up the preparation of the stuffing, blend all the stuffing ingredients in a food processor until almost paste-like.

INGREDIENTS

PREPARATION TIME
10 minutes
COOKING TIME
30 minutes

75 g (3 oz) streaky bacon, rind removed
1 small onion, peeled and chopped
10 g ($\frac{1}{2}$ oz) breadcrumbs
1 teaspoon dried sage or mixed herbs
grated rind and juice of $\frac{1}{2}$ lemon
Salt and finely ground black pepper
700g (1$\frac{1}{2}$ lb) whole grey mullet, cleaned and scaled
10 g ($\frac{1}{2}$ oz) butter

SEAFOOD CRUMBLE

SERVES

—— 4 ——

Savoury crumbles are great time-savers. They're as delicious as pastry-topped pies yet eliminate kneading and rolling, and they're hearty enough to enjoy without accompaniment unless you fancy a simple salad. This one is made using cod and prawns, topped with a deliciously buttery crumble.

INGREDIENTS

PREPARATION TIME
20 minutes
COOKING TIME
30 minutes

*350 g (12 oz) cod fillets,
skinned and boned
25 g (1 oz) butter
1 large onion, peeled and
sliced
1 tablespoon plain flour
350 ml (12 fl oz) milk
110 g (4 oz) button
mushrooms, halved
110 g (4 oz) frozen
prawns, thawed and
drained
Grated rind of 1 lemon
2 tablespoons capers,
roughly chopped
Salt and freshly ground
black pepper*

CRUMBLE
*150 g (5 oz) plain flour
75 g (3 oz) butter
2 tablespoons Parmesan
cheese, grated*

Pre-heat the oven to gas mark 5, 190°C (375°F).

Cut the cod into small pieces. Melt the butter in a saucepan, add the onion and fry for 2 minutes. Stir in the flour, then gradually add the milk. Bring to the boil and cook, stirring for 2 minutes or until thickened. Add the cod, mushrooms, prawns, lemon rind, capers and a little seasoning, mix well and pour into a shallow, ovenproof dish.

For the crumble, sift the flour into a bowl. Add the butter, cut into small pieces, and rub in with the fingertips until crumbly. Spoon over the fish mixture and sprinkle with the cheese. Bake for 35 minutes or until the crumble starts to turn golden. Serve immediately.

TIP

Crumbles are made in seconds in a food processor. Whizz the flour and butter together until the mixture resembles breadcrumbs.

WHOLE BAKED FISH IN FOIL

SERVES

—— 5-6 ——

There is something a little special about serving a whole baked fish. Once cooked, you simply lift it, still foil wrapped, onto a plate, open out the foil and tuck plenty of fresh herbs around the fish before carrying it to the dinner table.

'Carving' is slightly more difficult. The best method is to work up one side of the fish, removing suitably sized portions before turning the fish to attack the other fillet. If this bothers you, talk someone else into carving while you slip out to the kitchen to attend to the accompaniments!

As regards the choice of fish, salmon or bass is ideal, although I tested the recipe with an Arctic char, more trout-like in flavour but a good alternative and widely available in the autumn.

———

Pre-heat the oven to gas mark 5, 190°C (375°F).

Dot the centre of a large sheet of foil with half of the butter. Lay the cleaned fish over the butter. Drizzle with the lemon juice and put the lemon rind, bay leaves and some herbs inside the body cavity. Dot the salmon with the remaining butter and season lightly.

Bring the foil up over the fish and twist the ends together securely. Bake for 35 minutes. Open up the foil and test by piercing the thickest part of the fish through to the bone with the tip of a knife.

Transfer to a plate and garnish with fresh herbs. Serve with new potatoes and mangetout peas or a tossed salad and a sauce such as Hollandaise (p. 102) or garlic or herb mayonnaise.

INGREDIENTS

PREPARATION TIME
7 minutes
COOKING TIME
35 minutes

50 g (2 oz) butter
900 g (2 lb) whole salmon
Grated rind and juice of $\frac{1}{2}$ lemon
2 bay leaves
A handful of fresh herbs, e.g. parsley, tarragon, dill
Salt and freshly ground black pepper
Fresh herbs to garnish

COD WITH GARLIC AND CREAM CHEESE

SERVES
— 4 —

A deliciously simple baked dish that you can prepare in advance and cook when you're ready to eat. The garlicky flavoured cream cheese is used to coat the fish before baking. Use a low fat cream cheese (but not cottage cheese) if preferred.

INGREDIENTS

PREPARATION TIME
7 minutes
COOKING TIME
25 minutes

700 g (1¹/₂ lb) cod or haddock fillet, skinned and boned
2 cloves garlic, peeled and crushed
4 spring onions, trimmed and chopped
225 g (8 oz) cream cheese
Salt and freshly ground black pepper
Grated rind of 1 lime or lemon
Coarsely chopped parsley

Pre-heat the oven to gas mark 4, 180°C (350°F).

Lightly oil a large, shallow ovenproof dish. Cut the fish into four even-sized pieces and lay slightly apart in the dish. Beat the garlic and onions into the cream cheese and season lightly. Dot the mixture over the fish and bake for 25 minutes until the fish is cooked through.

Sprinkle with the lime or lemon rind and parsley and serve with pasta and green vegetables.

ON THE HOB

The marvellous thing about fish cookery is its sheer versatility. Even when you've tried the classic soups, stews, pies and fries there's still a vast array of dishes that I have loosely categorised under the heading 'On The Hob'. Cooking in this way really accentuates the 'quick and easy' theme as thin fillets or bite-sized pieces of fish are cooked through in mere minutes – be wary of leaving the kitchen! So that the fish doesn't sit waiting, have any vegetables or salad dishes organised before you start cooking. The Paella, pasta and couscous dishes form complete meals in themselves.

MUSSELS WITH PASTA

S E R V E S
—— 4 ——

If you can get fresh pasta for this recipe, use it. If not, use dried tagliatelle, spaghetti, or any other pasta that you have in the store-cupboard. The 'sauce' is really no more than a quick and easy dressing, lightly spiced with a dash of Tabasco. Serve extra Tabasco at the table for those who want to hot it up.

INGREDIENTS

PREPARATION TIME
20 minutes
COOKING TIME
10–16 minutes

900 g (2 lb) cleaned fresh mussels
275 g (10 oz) fresh or dried tagliatelle
4 tablespoons olive oil
4 tablespoons tomato purée
½ teaspoon Tabasco sauce
1 bunch spring onions, trimmed and sliced
2 cloves garlic, peeled and crushed
1 × 225 g (8 oz) can of pimientos, drained and roughly chopped
Salt and freshly ground black pepper

Bring 50 ml (2 fl oz) water to the boil in a large saucepan. Add the mussels, cover with a lid and cook for 3–4 minutes, shaking the pan frequently, until the mussels have opened. Drain the mussels, discarding any that remain closed. Remove and discard roughly half of the shells.

Cook the pasta in plenty of boiling salted water, allowing 3–4 minutes for fresh pasta and 8–10 minutes for dried. Drain.

Beat the oil with the tomato purée and Tabasco sauce. Return the pasta to a large saucepan with the mussels, spring onions, garlic, pimientos and dressing. Cook for about 2 minutes, tossing the ingredients lightly together. Season to taste and serve hot.

Opposite: PLAICE WITH CHORIZO STUFFING (PAGE 60)
Overleaf: HADDOCK WITH STRINGY CHEESE & PEPPER COULIS (PAGE 75)

TUNA COUSCOUS

S E R V E S
— 4 —

Wheat-based cereal products – couscous, bulgar, burghul or cracked wheat – all make welcome alternatives to potatoes, rice and pasta, either as part of a dish or as an accompaniment. Whichever you spot first in the supermarket or health food store can be topped with a deliciously rich fresh tuna sauce.

To save time, I've used a bottled sauce for pasta in this recipe, also available from supermarkets, which is perfectly acceptable. Check the ingredients list before you buy to make sure it contains no artificial ingredients. Shark steaks or swordfish can be used instead of tuna.

Place the couscous in a large bowl. Cover with plenty of cold water and leave to soak while preparing the sauce.

Cut the tuna into chunks. Melt 25 g (1 oz) of the butter in a large saucepan. Add the garlic, onions, carrots and pine nuts and cook gently for no more than 5 minutes. Stir in the tuna, mushrooms, pasta sauce and 5 tablespoons water. Cook gently, stirring frequently, for 10 minutes.

Drain the couscous and place in a separate saucepan with 4 tablespoons water. Cover and cook gently for 5 minutes until heated through. Stir in the parsley, remaining butter and seasoning, and spoon onto serving plates. Season the tuna sauce to taste and spoon over the couscous.

TIP

Couscous quickly turns to a stodgy paste if overcooked. Stir lightly during cooking, removing from the hob once heated through.

INGREDIENTS

PREPARATION TIME
20 minutes
COOKING TIME
21 minutes

350 g (12 oz) couscous
450 g (1 lb) fresh tuna,
skinned and boned
40 g (1½ oz) butter
3 cloves garlic, peeled and
crushed
2 medium onions, peeled
and chopped
4 carrots, chopped
50 g (2 oz) pine nuts
225 g (8 oz) small button
mushrooms
1 × 225 g (8 oz) bottle of
tomato and herb sauce for
pasta
6 tablespoons chopped fresh
parsley
Salt and freshly ground
black pepper

Opposite: TEMPURA (PAGE 91)
Preceding page: 'QUICK AND EASY' PAELLA (PAGE 79)

NORMANDY SOLE SAUTÉ

S E R V E S
—— 4 ——

INGREDIENTS

PREPARATION TIME
10 minutes
COOKING TIME
9 minutes

25 g (1 oz) butter
1 bunch of spring onions,
trimmed and sliced
2 small, red-skinned eating
apples, cored and sliced
8 large fillets of lemon sole,
skinned
250 ml (8 fl oz) medium
cider
4 tablespoons crème fraîche
Salt and freshly ground
black pepper

You can save enormously on preparation time by using ready-skinned flat fish. Supermarkets now sell prepared fish, and a friendly fishmonger will skin fillets for you, particularly if it's choice sole. (Plaice can be substituted.) Crème fraîche, a French soured cream product, adds a light creaminess to the sauce. Alternatively substitute 2 tablespoons of double cream.

———

Melt the butter in a large frying pan. Add the onions and apples and fry for 2–3 minutes until beginning to colour. Push the apples and onions to one side of the pan.

Add the sole fillets to the pan, folding each fillet in half so it takes up less room. Add the cider and bring just to the boil. Reduce heat, cover the pan with a lid or foil and cook for about 3 minutes until the fish has turned white.

Drain the fish to warmed serving plates. Add the crème fraîche to the pan and heat through gently. Season lightly and spoon over the fish. Serve hot with rice and a green vegetable.

ORIENTAL FONDUE

S E R V E S

—— 4 ——

When you're looking for something a little different to serve for a supper party, and you have access to a good supply of fresh fish, this recipe could be the perfect choice. A mixture of uncooked white fish, such as cod, haddock, halibut, whiting or monkfish, and shellfish is put on the table, along with a fondue pot of aromatic stock, so that the guests can cook pieces of fish, a few at a time. The spicy peanut sauce, a simple crisp salad and some nice bread is all that's required to complete this really 'fun' meal.

———

Cut the white fish into bite-sized pieces. Arrange the fish and shellfish on a large serving plate or on four small plates if you prefer a portion by each place setting. Cover loosely and chill until ready to serve.

Add the ginger, garlic, spring onions, celery, soy sauce and freshly boiled water to saucepan and return to the boil. Reduce the heat and simmer gently while preparing the sauce.

Heat the oil in a small saucepan and fry the spring onions and chilli for 1 minute. Stir in the soy sauce, peanut butter and water. Bring to the boil, reduce heat and simmer gently for about 5 minutes until thickened. Turn into a small serving dish.

Strain the stock into a fondue pot and position over the flame at the table. Provide fondue forks or skewers so that the guests can cook a few pieces of fish at a time in the stock.

TIP

An oriental-style food warming tray makes a good substitute for a fondue pot. Use a small heatproof dish on the tray for the stock, and return it to the hob for a quick blast if it starts to cool down.

INGREDIENTS

PREPARATION TIME
20 minutes
COOKING TIME
16 minutes

350 g (12 oz) fresh white fish fillets, skinned and boned
225 g (8 oz) prepared squid, sliced into rings
100 g (4 oz) large peeled prawns
100 g (4 oz) cooked mussels

STOCK

40 g (1½ oz) fresh root ginger, peeled and grated
3 cloves garlic, peeled and crushed
½ bunch spring onions, trimmed and sliced
2 celery stalks, sliced
2 tablespoons dark soy sauce
900 ml (1½ pints) water, freshly boiled

SAUCE

1 tablespoon vegetable oil
½ bunch spring onions, trimmed and thinly sliced
1 green or red chilli, de-seeded and finely chopped
1 tablespoon dark soy sauce
3 tablespoons peanut butter
150 ml (5 fl oz) water

KEDGEREE
WITH CRUSHED SPICES

SERVES
— 4 —

Although traditionally served as a breakfast or brunch dish, Kedgeree can be enhanced with cream and spices to make a delicious main meal. Use a coffee grinder or pestle and mortar to crush the spices. Failing this, pound the spices in a small bowl with the end of a rolling pin.

INGREDIENTS

PREPARATION TIME
15 minutes
COOKING TIME
23 minutes

275 g (10 oz) long-grain rice
4 eggs
450 g (1 lb) smoked haddock or cod
2 teaspoons fennel seeds
1 teaspoon cumin seeds
1 teaspoon coriander seeds
25 g (1 oz) butter
1 onion, peeled and sliced
¼ teaspoon ground turmeric
1 cinnamon stick, halved
85 ml (3 fl oz) single cream
Salt and freshly ground black pepper

Bring a pan of salted water to the boil. Add the rice and the whole eggs in their shells. Cook for 10 minutes until the rice is tender, then drain. Shell the eggs and cut into slices.

Place the fish in a frying pan with 2 tablespoons water. Cover and cook very gently for 5 minutes. Drain the fish reserving any juices. Roughly flake the fish, discarding the skin and any bones.

Lightly crush the spices. Melt the butter in a large saucepan. Add the onion, seeds, turmeric and cinnamon and fry gently for 5 minutes.

Stir in the rice, eggs, fish and cooking juices, and cream. Cook gently for 2 minutes until heated through. Season lightly and serve hot.

HADDOCK WITH STRINGY CHEESE AND PEPPER COULIS

SERVES
— 4 —

The creamy whiteness of the fish against the colourful mixture of peppers makes a beautiful contrast in both colour and flavour. Fillets of any white fish (e.g. cod) can be substituted for the steaks, but remember to reduce the cooking time.

For the coulis, heat the oil in a saucepan. Add the peppers, chilli powder, tomatoes and tomato juice and bring to the boil. Reduce heat, cover and cook gently for 5 minutes.

Grease a large heatproof, shallow dish with a little of the butter. Arrange the fillets in the dish. Dot with the remaining butter and season lightly. Cook under a moderate grill for 10 minutes. Turn the steaks over.

Arrange the cheese over the steaks. Return to the grill for 10 minutes until the cheese is bubbling and melted.

Lightly season the sauce and spoon onto serving plates. Arrange the fish over the sauce and garnish with the coriander. Serve hot with jacket potatoes.

INGREDIENTS

PREPARATION TIME
10 minutes
COOKING TIME
27 minutes

COULIS
1 tablespoon olive oil
1 red pepper, de-seeded and diced
1 yellow or orange pepper, de-seeded and diced
$\frac{1}{2}$ teaspoon chilli powder
1 × 225 g (8 oz) can chopped tomatoes
150 ml (5 fl oz) tomato juice

5 g ($\frac{1}{4}$ oz) butter
4 haddock steaks
Salt and freshly ground black pepper
75 g (3 oz) or 4 thin slices Emmenthal or Gruyère cheese
1 tablespoon chopped fresh coriander for garnish

SEAFOOD BREDY

SERVES
— 4 —

This simple recipe is based on a South African dish in which meat is cooked in a spicy, tomato 'stew'. Fish provides a lighter, yet none the less delicious variation.

Cut the fish into bite-sized pieces.

Heat the oil in a large saucepan, and fry the onions, garlic, chilli, bay leaves, cinnamon sticks and sugar gently for about 5 minutes until beginning to colour.

Add the tomatoes and white fish. Cover with lid and cook for 5 minutes. Add the prawns and season lightly. Serve hot with crusty bread and a green salad.

INGREDIENTS

PREPARATION TIME
10 minutes
COOKING TIME
11 minutes

700 g (1½ lb) cod, haddock or coley, skinned and boned
4 tablespoons vegetable oil
2 medium onions, peeled and sliced
2 cloves garlic, peeled and crushed
1 green or red chilli, de-seeded and chopped
4 bay leaves
3 cinnamon sticks, halved
1 tablespoon muscovado sugar
1 × 400 g (14 oz) can chopped tomatoes
100 g (4 oz) peeled prawns
Salt and freshly ground black pepper

NUTTY FISH DUMPLINGS

SERVES

— 4 —

I find the texture of huss too mushy to enjoy on its own, but perfect for fish cakes. I've called these 'dumplings' rather than cakes because of the way they're haphazardly shaped and rolled in flaked almonds, rather than carefully patted and coated in egg and breadcrumbs. The parsnips add a deliciously sweet flavour but potatoes can easily be substituted. Cod, coley and haddock can be substituted for huss.

Cook the parsnips in boiling salted water for 10–15 minutes until tender; drain.

Melt the butter in a frying pan and fry the huss gently for 3 minutes on each side. Purée the parsnips and huss in a food processor. (Alternatively, mash the parsnips then beat in the flaked huss.) Beat in the ground almonds, egg and seasoning. Roughly divide the mixture into eight.

Sprinkle the flaked almonds onto a plate. Spoon up an eighth of the fish mixture and roll it in the almonds. Repeat with the remaining mixture.

Heat the oil in the frying pan and add the dumplings. Fry for 1–2 minutes on each side until turning golden. Drain lightly on kitchen paper and serve with a tomato salad.

INGREDIENTS

PREPARATION TIME
15 minutes
COOKING TIME
23 minutes

---

225 g (8 oz) parsnips, peeled and cut into chunks
10 g (½ oz) butter
450 g (1 lb) huss, boned
50 g (2 oz) ground almonds
1 egg
Salt and freshly ground black pepper
50 g (2 oz) flaked almonds
vegetable oil for shallow frying

MINTED MONKFISH

S E R V E S

—— 4 ——

A s lovely as rich, creamy sauces are with most kinds of fish, yoghurt sauce makes a refreshing change. A subtle sprinkling of mint completes the 'fresh' theme.

Blend the cornflour with 1 tablespoon water, then mix with the yoghurt.

Melt the butter in a frying pan. Add the leeks and cook, stirring for 1 minute. Add the monkfish and cook for 2 minutes. Stir in the mangetouts (or peas) and wine. Bring to the boil, reduce heat and cover with lid or foil. Cook gently for 5 minutes.

Stir in the yoghurt mixture, mint and seasoning. Heat through for 2 minutes until slightly thickened. Serve hot with pasta or new potatoes.

INGREDIENTS

PREPARATION TIME
15 minutes
COOKING TIME
11 minutes

½ teaspoon cornflour
3 tablespoons Greek
yoghurt
25 g (1 oz) butter
1 large leek, thinly sliced
550 g (1¼ lb) monkfish,
boned and cut into bite-
sized pieces
75 g (3 oz) mangetout
peas, trimmed and halved,
or peas
85 ml (3 fl oz) medium
white wine
1 tablespoon chopped
fresh mint
Salt and freshly ground
black pepper

'QUICK AND EASY' PAELLA

S E R V E S
—— 4 - 6 ——

Making a traditional paella is quite an involved process. This shortcut version is equally tasty, if not as authentic as one you might have in a Spanish restaurant; however, I have retained the mussels, squid and saffron, three of the most crucial components in a really good paella.

Place the saffron in a small bowl with 2 tablespoons boiling water and leave to stand. Cut the fish into 4 portions.

Heat the oil in a large, shallow pan. Add onion and garlic and fry for 2 minutes. Push to one side of the pan.

Add the squid to the pan and fry until it turns white; drain. Add the bay leaves and rice to the pan and fry, stirring for 1 minute.

Add the saffron, stock or water and sausage. Bring to the boil. Reduce the heat and cover with a lid. Cook gently for about 10 minutes until the rice is just tender.

Tuck the white fish into the rice. Arrange the prawns and mussels over the rice. Re-cover with lid or foil and cook for a further 5 minutes until the fish is cooked and the mussels have opened. Serve hot.

INGREDIENTS

PREPARATION TIME
20–25 minutes
COOKING TIME
22 minutes

1 teaspoon saffron strands
450 g (1 lb) cod, coley or haddock fillet, skinned and boned
4 tablespoons olive oil
1 large onion, peeled and sliced
4 cloves garlic, peeled and crushed
450 g (1 lb) prepared squid, thinly sliced
2 bay leaves
275 g (10 oz) long-grain rice
600 ml (1 pint) stock (see page 16) or water
100 g (4 oz) chorizo or kabanos sausage, roughly sliced
8 king prawns
300 ml (10 fl oz) cleaned fresh mussels

SKATE IN PESTO

SERVES

—— 4 ——

Shop-bought pesto, an Italian basil and pine nut sauce, makes a great store-cupboard standby for enlivening casseroles, salads, pasta or, in this case, skate wings. Use it sparingly at first – it has a pleasant yet distinctive herby flavour.

INGREDIENTS

PREPARATION TIME
5 minutes
COOKING TIME
17 minutes

---

2 large or 4 small skate wings
10 g (½ oz) butter
1 teaspoon vegetable oil
1–2 teaspoons pesto
150 ml (5 fl oz) double cream
2 tablespoons chopped fresh parsley
Salt and freshly ground black pepper
1 tablespoon pine nuts, toasted

If using large skate wings chop them in half by placing the thick end of a heavy knife over the thickest area of the cartilage and beating sharply with a rolling pin or hammer.

Melt the butter with the oil in a large frying pan. Add the skate and fry gently for 10 minutes. Turn the fish over and cook for a further 5 minutes. Drain to warmed serving plates.

Stir the pesto, cream, parsley and 2 tablespoons water into the pan juices and heat through gently for 1 minute. Season lightly. Pour the sauce over the fish and sprinkle with the pine nuts. Serve hot with sautéed potatoes and a green vegetable.

PEPPERED SALMON STEAKS

S E R V E S

—— 4 ——

Cooking fish *au poivre* works just as well as with any meat steaks. Look out for Sichuan pepper on supermarket herb and spice racks. It's not as hot as ordinary pepper, but has a slightly aniseed flavour that complements fish perfectly. If you can't get hold of any don't give up on this recipe – simply substitute crushed black peppercorns.

Sprinkle 1 tablespoon of the pepper over the tops of the salmon steaks. Press lightly into the flesh with the fingers. Turn the steaks over and cover with the remaining pepper.

Melt the butter with the oil in a frying pan. Add the salmon and fry very gently for 5 minutes. Turn the steaks over and add the wine or water. Cover the pan with a lid or foil and cook gently for a further 7–10 minutes. Drain the salmon and place on warmed serving plates.

Add the cream to the pan juices and bring to the boil. Stir for 1 minute and season lightly. Spoon around the salmon and serve hot with new potatoes and mangetout or broccoli.

INGREDIENTS

PREPARATION TIME
10 minutes
COOKING TIME
16 minutes

2 tablespoons Sichuan pepper
4 salmon steaks, about 2 cm (¾ in) thick
25 g (1 oz) butter
1 teaspoon vegetable oil
50 ml (2 fl oz) medium white wine or water
85 ml (3 fl oz) double cream
Salt and freshly ground black pepper

SEAFOOD CURRY

S E R V E S

— 6 —

INGREDIENTS

PREPARATION TIME
15 minutes
COOKING TIME
25 minutes

5 tablespoons vegetable oil
3 onions, peeled and
chopped
5 cm (2 in) piece fresh root
ginger, peeled and grated
2 cloves garlic, peeled and
crushed
1 large fresh chilli,
de-seeded and finely
chopped or 2 dried chillis,
crumbled
3 bay leaves
1 tablespoon ground cumin
1 tablespoon ground
coriander
1 tablespoon fennel seeds
½ teaspoon ground turmeric
1 teaspoon ground allspice
50 g (2 oz) creamed
coconut
450 ml (15 fl oz) water
2 medium potatoes, peeled
and cut into chunks
900 g (2 lb) mixture of
white fish, skinned, boned
and cut into chunks
100 g (4 oz) peeled
prawns
4 tablespoons double cream
Salt and freshly ground
black pepper
Bay leaves for garnish

Considering that this curry is put together quickly using readily available ingredients, it tastes remarkably authentic. Most of the spices used are the ready-ground variety, fried in oil to bring out their flavour, but you can substitute whole spices, allowing an extra teaspoon of each. The choice of fish is infinitely flexible. Use any reasonably priced, firm-textured white fish such as cod, haddock, coley, shark or swordfish.

Heat the oil in a large saucepan. Add the onions, ginger, garlic, chilli, bay leaves and spices and fry for 5 minutes.

Add the creamed coconut and water and bring to the boil.

Add the potatoes and cook, covered with a lid, for 10 minutes.

Add the white fish and cook for 5 minutes. Stir in the prawns and cream and season to taste. Cook gently for a further 5 minutes.

Spoon onto plates, garnish with bay leaves and serve with plain boiled rice.

DEVILLED COLEY

S E R V E S
—— 4 ——

A hot, tangy 'devilled' glaze is perfect for adding colour and flavour to cheap, bland fish such as coley. Serve with rice and a salad for a fast midweek filler. Cod or haddock can be substituted for coley.

Mix together the Worcester sauce, mustard, chutney and fruit juice.

Melt the butter in a frying pan. Add the coley and fry for 3 minutes. Turn the fish over and spread with the sauce. Cook for a further 3 minutes. Season lightly.

INGREDIENTS

PREPARATION TIME
3 minutes
COOKING TIME
6 minutes

1 tablespoon Worcester sauce
1 tablespoon grainy mustard
1 tablespoon mango chutney
2 tablespoons fresh orange or apple juice
25 g (1 oz) butter
4 small coley fillets, skinned and boned
Salt and freshly ground black pepper

TROUT WITH TANGY RASPBERRY SAUCE

SERVES
—— 4 ——

PREPARATION TIME
8 minutes
COOKING TIME
13 minutes

4 trout fillets
15 g (¹/₂ oz) butter
Salt and freshly ground
black pepper
350 g (12 oz) fresh or
frozen raspberries
1¹/₂ teaspoons white wine
vinegar
5 teaspoons redcurrant jelly
1 teaspoon grainy mustard

Steaming fish preserves the flavour and texture and requires no special equipment. I place the fish on a wire rack, set over a frying pan of simmering water and covered with a lid of foil. Trout fillets, served with a tangy fruit sauce, make a healthy and refreshing meal.

Lay the trout fillets on a wire cooling rack or grill rack and dot with the butter. Season lightly.

Place the rack over a large frying pan of simmering water. Cover the rack with foil and steam the fish for 10 minutes or until the fish is cooked. Test the thickest part of one fillet with a knife.

Reserve 75 g (3 oz) of the raspberries. Press the remainder through a sieve into a small pan. Add the vinegar, redcurrant jelly, mustard and a little seasoning and cook gently until the jelly has melted and the sauce is hot.

Transfer the fish to warmed plates. Add the remaining raspberries to the sauce and immediately spoon around the fish. Serve with new potatoes and mangetout.

TIP

The sharpness of the sauce will depend on the sweetness of the raspberries used. Add a little more redcurrant jelly if they are particularly sharp.

Penne with Smoked Salmon

S E R V E S

— 4 —

Nothing could be quicker or more delicious than this simple blend of smoked salmon, cream and pasta. It is ideal for a festive brunch, summer lunch or late supper, but remember to keep portions fairly small as, not surprisingly, it's pretty rich!

Cook the pasta in plenty of boiling salted water for 8–10 minutes until just tender, drain. Roughly shred the salmon.

Gently heat the cream in a saucepan with the lime or lemon rind and a little seasoning. Add the salmon and pasta and heat through for 1 minute. Serve sprinkled with dill or parsley.

INGREDIENTS

PREPARATION TIME
10 minutes
COOKING TIME
10–12 minutes

300 g (10 oz) penne pasta
225 g (8 oz) smoked salmon
225 ml (8 fl oz) double cream
Grated rind of 1 lime or lemon
Salt and freshly ground black pepper
2 tablespoons chopped dill or parsley

SKATE AND MUSHROOM GRATIN

S E R V E S

—— 3 - 4 ——

Tossed in a simple sauce of creamy yoghurt, tomato purée and mayonnaise, sweet and succulent skate takes on an almost shellfish-like flavour. This recipe uses just one large skate wing to give three to four deliciously rich servings. For particularly hearty appetites serve jacket potatoes or crusty bread.

Place the skate in a pan with 4 tablespoons water. Cover and cook gently for 3 minutes. Turn the skate over and cook for a further 3 minutes. Drain and shred the flesh away from the cartilage.

Melt the butter in a pan. Fry the mushrooms and spring onions for 1 minute. Season to taste. Turn into a shallow flameproof serving dish.

Beat together the yoghurt, mayonnaise and tomato purée and season to taste. Stir in the skate. Spoon the mixture over the mushrooms and sprinkle with the breadcrumbs. Cook under a low grill for about 7 minutes until the breadcrumbs are turning golden. Serve hot.

INGREDIENTS

PREPARATION TIME
15 minutes
COOKING TIME
14 minutes

*1 large skate wing (about
450g/1 lb)
25 g (1 oz) butter
225 g (8 oz) button
mushrooms, roughly sliced
1 bunch spring onions,
trimmed and sliced
Salt and freshly ground
black pepper
100 g (4 oz) Greek
yoghurt
2 tablespoons mayonnaise
1 tablespoon tomato purée
25 g (1 oz) breadcrumbs*

FRIES AND STIR FRIES

Of all the different ways of cooking fish, fried is the method that most often springs to mind. Not the home-cooked version, but 'chip-shop' fish, smothered in a thick layer of batter and deep fried, sometimes with delicious results, at other times not so good.

In this chapter I've included, as well as crisp, airy Japanese Tempura, one fish in batter recipe, delicious enough to satisfy fried-fish lovers, but at the same time light enough to appeal to the more health conscious. Achieving good results lies as much in the technique as in the recipe. Heating the oil to the right temperature is crucial. To test whether the oil is at the right temperature drop a little batter into it – it should rise to the surface and sizzle. Once the fish has been added, don't forget to regulate the temperature. The oil, if kept over a high heat, will crisp up the batter before the fish has cooked through. At the other extreme, if the oil is insufficiently heated the batter will absorb the oil, producing soggy results. Once the fish is cooked, always drain it thoroughly on kitchen paper before serving.

Also included in this chapter are some pan-fries, shallow-fries and stir-fry dishes. These stir-fries rely on minimum oil, intense heat and fast cooking to produce crisp, tasty, quick and easy dishes.

PARMESAN AND PRAWN BEIGNETS

S E R V E S

—— 4 ——

PREPARATION TIME
10 minutes
COOKING TIME
6–8 minutes

50 g (2 oz) plain flour
1 egg
2 teaspoons vegetable oil
100 ml (4 fl oz) milk
175 g (6 oz) peeled
prawns, drained and
roughly chopped
25 g (1 oz) Parmesan
cheese
Oil for deep-frying

Like most deep-fried nibbles, these crisp, airy fritters are irresistible, but also very rich. So that you can serve them fresh from the fryer, have everything else ready first – a mixed salad is ideal for a lunchtime accompaniment. This quantity will stretch to serve six as a starter. For a useful store-cupboard variation, substitute a small, drained can of cockles or clams, or a drained and chopped can of anchovies.

Place the flour in a bowl and make a well in the centre. Separate the egg and put the white in a separate bowl. Add the yolk to the flour with the oil and a little of the milk. Whisk together, gradually incorporating the flour to make a smooth batter. Stir in the remaining milk, prawns and cheese.

Whisk the white until stiff. Using a tablespoon fold the white into the batter.

Heat a 5 cm (2 in) depth of oil in a deep frying-pan until a drop of the batter sizzles on the surface. Take dessertspoons of the prawns in batter and fry, several at a time, until golden on the underside. Turn over to brown the other sides. Drain on kitchen paper and keep warm while cooking the remainder.

Cod steaks
with tartare butter

S E R V E S

— 4 —

The classic 'tartare' threesome – gherkins, capers and parsley – is used here to zip up a simple dish of fried cod. For presentation choose neat, compact pieces of cod or substitute haddock, salmon, shark or swordfish steaks if they look a better buy.

Thoroughly dry the cod on kitchen paper, then coat with the flour.

Melt half the butter with the oil in a large frying-pan. Fry the fish steaks gently for 8 minutes. Turn fish over and cook for a further 6–8 minutes until cooked through. Drain the fish and place on warmed serving plates.

Add the remaining butter to the pan with the capers, gherkins, parsley and lemon juice. Season well and cook gently for 1 minute. Spoon around the fish and serve hot with new potatoes and a green vegetable.

INGREDIENTS

PREPARATION TIME
10 minutes
COOKING TIME
15–17 minutes

4 cod steaks
1½ teaspoons plain flour
50 g (2 oz) butter
2 tablespoons vegetable oil
3 tablespoons capers, finely chopped
10 small gherkins, finely chopped
4 tablespoons chopped parsley
2 teaspoons lemon juice
Salt and freshly ground black pepper

SIZZLING SHARK

S E R V E S

—— 3 - 4 ——

Light on bones and meaty in texture, shark makes an ideal choice for shredding and stir-frying. Here it is tossed in a hot chilli sauce then spooned onto a bed of chilled iceberg lettuce for a dramatic contrast in texture and flavour. Don't be put off if you cannot buy shark: swordfish or any other firm-textured white fish can be treated in the same way, even cod or haddock if you cube rather than shred the fish. You could also serve this dish as a starter – this quantity would serve six people.

Place the lettuce in a bowl or bag and chill while preparing the shark.

Slice the shark flesh as thinly as possible.

Heat the oil in a large frying-pan and fry the spring onions and chilli powder for 1 minute. Add the fish and fry, turning constantly, for 3 minutes. Stir in the red pepper, ginger, soy sauce and lemon or lime juice and cook for 30 seconds.

Transfer the lettuce to serving plates and spoon the fish mixture over it. Serve immediately.

INGREDIENTS

PREPARATION TIME
15 minutes
COOKING TIME
5 minutes

*1 small iceberg lettuce,
halved and shredded*
*700 g (1½ lb) shark steaks,
skinned and boned*
*2 tablespoons sesame or
vegetable oil*
*1 bunch spring onions,
trimmed and sliced*
½ teaspoon chilli powder
*½ red pepper, de-seeded and
shredded*
*1 piece stem ginger (about
10 g/½ oz), cut into slivers*
*2 tablespoons light soy
sauce*
*1 tablespoon lemon or
lime juice*

TEMPURA

S E R V E S

—— 4 ——

Tempura is a Japanese dish in which daintily cut pieces of fish and vegetables are deep-fried in a batter that is so fine, both fish and vegetables are clearly visible through it. It is accompanied by a hot dipping sauce, making a complete, light meal or an interesting starter. For best results, make the batter just before frying, and don't overcrowd the pan – cook just a few at a time.

Remove the heads and shells from the prawns, leaving the tails intact. Cut the plaice into thin strips. Cut away the cartilage and thinly slice the monkfish.

To make the sauce, mix the ginger and chilli with the soy sauce and sherry.

To make the batter, beat the egg in a bowl with 100 ml (4 fl oz) cold water. Gradually whisk in the flour and $\frac{1}{2}$ teaspoon of the oil.

Heat the oil in a deep frying-pan until a little of the batter sizzles on the surface. Dip the fish and vegetables, a few at a time, into the batter, and fry until pale golden. Drain on kitchen paper and keep warm while cooking the remainder.

Serve the fish and vegetables hot, with the dipping sauce.

TIP

Divide the sauce between very small bowls, ramekins or even egg cups and set each on a serving plate.

INGREDIENTS

PREPARATION TIME
15 minutes
COOKING TIME
5–10 minutes

12 king prawns
225 g (8 oz) plaice or lemon sole fillet, skinned
225 g (8 oz) monkfish
1 red or orange pepper, de-seeded and cut into thin strips
50 g (2 oz) mangetouts, trimmed
100 g (4 oz) button mushrooms, halved if necessary

DIPPING SAUCE
2.5 cm (1 in) piece fresh root ginger, peeled and grated
$\frac{1}{2}$ small chilli, de-seeded and finely chopped
85 ml (3 fl oz) dark soy sauce
25 ml (1 fl oz) medium sherry

BATTER
1 egg
100 ml (4 fl oz) water
100 g (4 oz) plain flour
$\frac{1}{2}$ teaspoon vegetable oil

Oil for deep-frying

SWORDFISH WITH CARAMELISED LEMON

SERVES
— 4 —

V irtually bone-free, meaty swordfish is a treat you can really tuck into. Enhance its flavour with this sweet, tangy and buttery glaze. Shark steaks can be substituted.

INGREDIENTS

PREPARATION TIME
5 minutes
COOKING TIME
12 minutes

50 g (2 oz) butter
1 tablespoon vegetable oil
1 tablespoon caster sugar
1½ lemons, thinly sliced
4 small swordfish steaks
Juice of ½ lemon
Salt and freshly ground
black pepper
1 tablespoon chopped fresh
parsley

Melt the butter with the oil in a large frying-pan. Sprinkle the sugar over and add the lemon slices. Fry gently for 3 minutes. Turn over the slices and push to one side of the pan.

Add the fish steaks and fry for 3 minutes. Turn the steaks over and arrange the lemon slices over them. Fry for a further 5 minutes. Drain the swordfish and lemon slices; place on serving plates and keep warm.

Add the lemon juice to the pan with 4 tablespoons water and seasoning. Bring to the boil, stirring, and pour over the steaks. Sprinkle with the parsley and serve with chips or jacket potatoes and a watercress salad.

Minced fish and Mangetout stir-fry

SERVES
— 4 —

Just like minced beef, fish can be finely minced or chopped and patted into balls for frying. Served on a bed of noodles with a colourful selection of crispy vegetables, it makes an 'out of the ordinary' supper dish.

Blend the fish, spring onions and bacon in a food processor to a paste. (Alternatively, chop the ingredients finely on a chopping board.)

Beat in 2 teaspoons soy sauce and the egg white. Roughly shape into balls about 2.5 cm (1 in) in diameter.

Heat the oil in a frying-pan. Fry the fish balls, turning frequently, for 7 minutes until turning golden. Drain and wipe out the pan.

Add a little extra oil to the pan and fry the pepper, mangetout, ginger and garlic for 2 minutes.

Blend the cornflour with a little water in a measuring jug. Make up to 150 ml (5 fl oz) with water. Stir in the lemon juice, sherry and remaining soy sauce.

Return the fish balls to the pan with the cornflour mixture and cook gently for 2 minutes until the sauce has thickened.

Serve on a bed of noodles.

INGREDIENTS

PREPARATION TIME
20 minutes
COOKING TIME
11 minutes

450 g (1 lb) cod or haddock, skinned, boned and cut into chunks
½ bunch spring onions, trimmed and sliced
3 rashers streaky bacon, rind removed, chopped
2 tablespoons light soy sauce
1 egg white
2 tablespoons vegetable oil
1 orange or red pepper, de-seeded and sliced
225 g (8 oz) mangetout, trimmed
2.5 cm (1 in) piece fresh root ginger, peeled and grated
1 clove garlic, peeled and crushed
1 teaspoon cornflour
Juice of ½ lemon
2 tablespoons medium sherry

DEEP-FRIED FISH IN COCONUT

SERVES

—— 4 ——

INGREDIENTS

PREPARATION TIME
10 minutes
COOKING TIME
4 minutes

450 g (1 lb) whiting, cod,
haddock or plaice fillets,
skinned and boned
Flour for coating, seasoned
with salt and freshly
ground black pepper
1 egg
100 g (4 oz) desiccated
coconut
Oil for deep-frying
Mango chutney for serving

Desiccated coconut has all the coating and frying qualities of the more commonly used breadcrumbs, but has the added advantage that it comes ready to use. For a spicy flavour, add a sprinkling of curry powder to the coconut before coating the fish.

Cut the fish into 1 cm ($\frac{1}{2}$ in) wide strips and coat with flour. Lightly beat the egg. Dip the fish in the egg, then coat evenly in the coconut.

Heat the oil in a deep fryer until a little coconut sizzles on the surface. Add several pieces of fish and fry for 1 minute or until golden. Drain on kitchen paper and keep warm while frying the remainder.

Serve with the mango chutney and a cucumber salad.

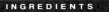

DEEP-FRIED HUSS

S E R V E S

—— 4 ——

A lighter version of the more traditional 'battered' fish. The turmeric is not essential but does add an appetising golden 'glow'. Small portions of cod, haddock, plaice, skate, whiting or coley can easily be used in place of the huss.

Cut the huss flesh away from the central bone, then divide into 4 equal portions.

Sift the flour, turmeric and a pinch of salt into a bowl. Make a well in the centre. Add a little of the milk to the well and gradually whisk in the flour to make a smooth batter. Beat in the remaining milk.

Heat the oil in a deep fryer or large saucepan until a drop of the batter sizzles on the surface. Dip two of the fish portions into the batter then lower into the oil. Cook for 3–4 minutes until golden, turning over half way through the cooking time. Drain on kitchen paper and keep warm while frying the remaining fish.

INGREDIENTS

PREPARATION TIME
10 minutes
COOKING TIME
6–8 minutes

700 g (1½ lb) huss
100 g (4 oz) plain flour
¼ teaspoon ground turmeric
A pinch of salt
250 ml (8 fl oz) milk
Oil for deep-frying

STIR-FRIED PRAWNS

S E R V E S
—— 3 - 4 ——

This is a fairly basic, yet none the less delicious, stir-fry dish with a light sweet-and-sour sauce. I've used prawns which can be stirred without falling apart, but you can substitute 350 g (12 oz) of white fish if you don't mind the pieces breaking up a little.

Coat the prawns in the cornflour.

Blend together the soy sauce, vinegar, sherry, honey and orange or apple juice.

Heat the oil in a large frying-pan or wok. Fry the spring onions, garlic and carrots, stirring for 1 minute. Add the mushrooms and cucumber and fry for 1 minute.

Drain the vegetables and add the prawns to the pan. Fry for 1 minute.

Return the vegetables to the pan with the sauce mixture. Heat through for 1–2 minutes. Serve hot with noodles or rice.

INGREDIENTS

PREPARATION TIME
15 minutes
COOKING TIME
4–5 minutes

225 g (8 oz) peeled prawns, drained
2 teaspoons cornflour
2 tablespoons soy sauce
1 tablespoon white wine vinegar
2 tablespoons medium sherry
2 tablespoons clear honey
85 ml (3 fl oz) orange or apple juice
2 tablespoons vegetable oil
1 bunch spring onions, trimmed and sliced
1 clove garlic, peeled and crushed
1 large carrot, cut into matchstick-sized lengths
100 g (4 oz) button mushrooms, trimmed
½ cucumber, peeled and cut into matchstick-sized lengths

Sprats with Mexican Crumbs

SERVES
— 4 —

A sprinkling of chilli seasoning and some crushed Mexican-style tortilla chips make a tasty and convenient alternative to breadcrumbs for coating small whole fish. Sprats, like whitebait, should be eaten on the day they are bought, and if you do this they don't need gutting.

Halve the avocado and remove the stone. Scoop the flesh into a bowl and mash with a fork. Add the lemon juice, grated onion, mayonnaise, curry powder and a little seasoning and continue mashing until fairly smooth. Transfer the mixture to a small serving bowl.

Wash and dry the sprats and coat with the egg. Place the tortilla chips and chilli seasoning in a polythene bag and finely crush with a rolling pin. Add the sprats to the polythene bag, about a quarter at a time and toss until coated in crumbs.

When all the sprats are coated heat a 5 mm ($^1/_4$ in) depth of oil in a large frying pan. Add half the sprats and fry for one minute on each side. Drain on kitchen paper and keep warm while frying the remainder. Serve hot with the avocado dip.

INGREDIENTS

PREPARATION TIME
10 minutes
COOKING TIME
4 minutes

1 ripe avocado
1 teaspoon lemon juice
1 tablespoon finely grated onion
1 tablespoon mayonnaise
$^1/_4$ teaspoon curry powder
Salt and freshly ground black pepper
450 g (1 lb) whole sprats
1 egg, beaten
75 g (3 oz) tortilla chips
$^1/_2$ teaspoon chilli seasoning
Oil for shallow frying

GRILLS AND BARBECUES

When you have bought a deliciously fresh piece of fish and are looking for the ultimate 'quick and easy' cooking technique, grilling certainly comes into its own. It is clean and fast, and retains maximum flavour and moisture. The following recipes are straightforward and include some simple toppings, glazes, savoury butters and basting sauces for cheering up almost any fish.

Unless using sardines or other small oily varieties, the fish should be gutted and scored down each side to speed up cooking and allow any sauces or marinades to penetrate. Take cooking times purely as a guide as this depends so much on the raw temperature of the fish, the speed of the grill and the distance of the fish from the heat source. When the fish starts to look cooked, pierce the thickest part through to the bone with a skewer or knife. If the flesh flakes easily it is done; if the juices run pink and the flesh clings to the bone, allow a little longer. Avoid overcooking, as the fish will be dry, tasteless and thoroughly disappointing to eat.

Barbecuing fish requires a little more practice and skill. While the preparation is the same as for grilling, extra care must be taken with the cooking. Floppy fillets, or small fish which might fall through the wide grill mesh, are best secured in a hinged, fish-shaped grip. Smaller fish can be cooked near the coals; large whole fish must be well raised so that the centre is cooked through before the surface burns. Use the same sauces and marinades as for grilling, but reduce oil or fat contents which can cause 'flaring'. Cooking times will also be reduced. It's a case of practice makes perfect!

COOKING TIMES FOR GRILLED FISH

Whether plain grilled, marinated or basted use the following cooking times for whole fish, fillets or steaks:

Whole Dover or lemon sole, or plaice	2 minutes per side
Skinned fillets of cod, haddock or coley	3 minutes per side
2 cm ($\frac{3}{4}$ in) steaks of salmon, cod, haddock or halibut	3 – 4 minutes per side
2 cm ($\frac{3}{4}$ in) steaks of shark, swordfish or tuna	5 – 6 minutes per side
Small whole fish, e.g. sardines, sprats	$1\frac{1}{2}$ minutes per side
Larger whole fish, e.g. mackerel, herrings, red mullet, trout	6 – 8 minutes per side

Basting marinades

These are great for adding flavour to prepared fish that you won't be cooking for another few hours. Whole fish, fillets or steaks can be steeped in the marinade, drained before grilling or barbecuing, and basted with the remaining marinade whilst cooking. Each marinade will be sufficient for 4–6 portions of fish.

Herb oil marinade

1 small onion, peeled and
chopped
2 cloves garlic, peeled and
sliced
A handful of mixed fresh
herbs, e.g. thyme,
rosemary, sage, parsley
6 tablespoons olive oil
2 tablespoons lemon juice
or white wine vinegar
Salt and freshly ground
black pepper

Blend all the ingredients together thoroughly.

Spiced yoghurt marinade

5 cm (2 in) piece fresh root
ginger, peeled and grated
2 cloves garlic, peeled and
crushed
½ teaspoon curry powder
¼ teaspoon chilli powder
2 tablespoons vegetable oil
150 ml (5 fl oz) natural
yoghurt
A pinch of salt

Blend all the ingredients together thoroughly.

TIP

If you don't have a handy supply of fresh herbs, buy a pack of mixed fresh herbs from the supermarket.

Savoury butters

A perfectly fresh piece of cod, haddock or sole, or even the more exotic species such as halibut or bass, needs little dressing up. Instead, try a pat of savoury butter which oozes its delicious flavour into the fish as it's carried to the table. The following butters will each cut into 10 slices and keep well in the fridge for up to a week. If stored for any longer, cut into portions and freeze in a bag so you can take out the portions as you need them.

Garlic, lemon and herb butter

2 cloves garlic, peeled and
crushed
100 g (4 oz) butter,
softened
2 tablespoons chopped fresh
herbs (e.g. parsley, chervil,
tarragon, basil, dill)
Grated rind of 1 lemon
Salt and freshly ground
black pepper

Beat the garlic into the butter with the herbs, lemon rind and a little seasoning.

Turn onto a piece of greaseproof paper and roll up in the paper, squeezing the butter into a log about 15 cm (6 in) long. Chill for at least 30 minutes. Cut slices about 1 cm ($\frac{1}{2}$ in) thick, and serve on grilled fish steaks, fillets or whole flat fish.

HAZELNUT BUTTER

Grated rind of 1 orange
50 g (2 oz) chopped
toasted hazelnuts
100 g (4 oz) butter,
softened

Beat the orange rind and hazelnuts into the butter. Continue as for Garlic, Lemon and Herb Butter.

ITALIAN BUTTER

5 stoned black or green
olives, finely chopped
100 g (4 oz) butter,
softened
2 teaspoons tomato purée
2 tablespoons grated
Parmesan cheese

Beat the olives into the butter with the tomato purée and Parmesan cheese. Continue as for Garlic, Lemon and Herb Butter.

HOLLANDAISE SAUCE

SERVES
—— 4-6 ——

A luxurious fish deserves a luxurious sauce and Hollandaise must be the perfect example. There are various 'shortcut' versions, but I find the classic method gives best results and takes little, if any, extra time to prepare.

There are several fish that can partner Hollandaise sauce. Steaks of salmon or halibut are ideal, or even really fresh cod or haddock. Butter, season and grill them while you prepare the sauce. Once made, Hollandaise sauce will sit quite happily over a pan of hot water, covered with a lid, for 20–30 minutes. Despite popular belief, it needn't be served at once.

Place the vinegar in a small pan and boil rapidly until reduced to 1 tablespoon. Transfer to a bowl with the egg yolks.

Rest the bowl over a saucepan of hot but not boiling water. Add the butter to the bowl, a little at a time, and whisk well after each addition until the sauce is smooth and thickly coats the back of a spoon. Add the lemon juice and seasoning to taste.

HERB HOLLANDAISE

Add 2 tablespoons chopped fresh dill or tarragon to the egg yolks.

ORANGE HOLLANDAISE

Add the finely grated rind of 1 orange to the egg yolks.

TIP

If the water gets too hot the sauce may curdle. If this happens beat in a tablespoon of very hot water. If this doesn't work start again with another egg yolk in a clean bowl and gradually add the 'failed' sauce.

GRILLED HERRINGS WITH SPINACH AND PINE NUTS (PAGE 106)

INGREDIENTS

PREPARATION TIME
5 minutes
COOKING TIME
5 minutes

3 tablespoons white wine vinegar
3 egg yolks
175 g (6 oz) butter, softened
A few drops of lemon juice
Salt and freshly ground black pepper

SALTED TROUT

SERVES

— 2 —

This recipe is lovely when you've got really fresh trout, preferably fairly small ones. The salty soy coating lightly flavours the flesh without giving an over-salty taste, unless you actually eat the skin. A lavish sprinkling of salt over the head and tail also gives a more appetising finish and prevents the tail catching under the grill.

───

Line the grill rack with foil, folding up edges to make a tray. Lightly brush the foil with oil. Mix together the soy sauce, lemon rind and black pepper and rub a little into the cavity of each trout.

Lay the trout on the foil and brush with half of the soy sauce mixture. Sprinkle each head and tail with plenty of salt, then sprinkle more cautiously over the body. Cook under a moderate grill for 6 minutes, reducing the heat if the trout start to burn. Turn the trout, brush with the remaining soy sauce mixture and salt in the same way. Cook for a further 6 minutes.

Transfer to warmed serving plates and pour over any cooking juices. Serve with a cucumber salad and rice or bread.

INGREDIENTS

PREPARATION TIME
3 minutes
COOKING TIME
12 minutes

2 teaspoons dark soy sauce
Finely grated rind of
¹/₂lemon
Salt and freshly ground
black pepper
2 small trout, each
weighing about 225 g
(8 oz), gutted

GINGERED TUNA AND GRAPE SALAD (PAGE 129)

GRILLED HERRINGS WITH SPINACH AND PINE NUTS

SERVES
— 4 —

Rich in oil, herrings make a perfect choice for grilling. In this recipe their flavour mingles perfectly with the spinach and pine nut stuffing. You could also buy filleted herrings and sandwich the stuffing between two fillets.

INGREDIENTS

PREPARATION TIME
12 minutes
COOKING TIME
19 minutes

4 small boned herrings or 8 small herring fillets
40 g (1½ oz) butter
1 small onion, peeled and chopped
225 g (8 oz) frozen spinach, thawed
25 g (1 oz) breadcrumbs
25 g (1 oz) Parmesan cheese, grated
25 g (1 oz) pine nuts
Salt and freshly ground black pepper

Make 3–4 cuts through the skin on each side of the herring fillets or whole herrings. Melt the butter and fry the onion for 3 minutes. Place the spinach in a sieve and press out the excess liquid. Mix the spinach, breadcrumbs, cheese, pine nuts and seasoning into the fried onion.

Spoon the spinach mixture into the boned herrings or between the fillets and place in a lightly greased heatproof dish. Cook under a moderate grill for 8 minutes. Carefully turn the fish and cook for a further 8 minutes until it flakes easily when the thickest part is pierced with a knife.

Serve with a tomato salad.

MACKEREL WITH GARLIC AND ORANGE BUTTER

SERVES
— 4 —

Fresh mackerel fillets are a recent addition to supermarket chilled fish cabinets. Easy to eat, they're perfectly proportioned for those who find a whole mackerel just too much to tackle. Grey mullet or tuna can be substituted for mackerel.

Lay the mackerel fillets, skin sides down, in a lightly greased shallow heatproof dish.

Grate the rind from the orange. Cut the skin away from the orange then, working over the mackerel to catch the juices, cut the orange flesh from between the segments. Lay the segments over the mackerel.

Beat the garlic, orange rind and seasoning into the butter. Dot over the mackerel and cook under a moderate grill for 5 minutes.

Serve hot with granary bread and a leafy salad.

INGREDIENTS

PREPARATION TIME
3 minutes
COOKING TIME
5 minutes

4 mackerel fillets
1 orange
1 clove garlic, peeled and crushed
Salt and freshly ground black pepper
25 g (1 oz) butter, softened

MONKFISH BROCHETTES

SERVES

—— 4-6 ——

PREPARATION TIME
10 minutes
COOKING TIME
6–8 minutes

700 g (1½ lb) monkfish
100 g (4 oz) rindless
smoked streaky bacon
2 tablespoons chopped fresh
chives, or finely chopped
spring onion tops
4 tablespoons vermouth
150 ml (5 fl oz) double
cream
Salt and finely ground
black pepper

Wrapping fish in bacon makes a foolproof way of retaining moisture and flavour, even under the intense heat of the grill. Here, pieces of monkfish are secured in bacon and threaded onto skewers for easy handling. Place a small roasting tin under the grill rack to catch the juices, and then transfer the tin to the hob to complete a creamy sauce accompaniment. For a barbecue version use a lean bacon instead of the streaky and, as you will lose the juices on the coals, serve a herb or mustard mayonnaise to take the place of the sauce.

Discard the cartilage from the monkfish and cut the fillet into chunks. Stretch the bacon with the back of a knife and cut each rasher widthways into three pieces. Sprinkle the chives or spring onion tops over the bacon and wrap around the fish. Thread onto four to six long metal or wooden skewers.

Place a roasting tin under the grill rack. Lay the brochettes over the rack and cook under a moderate heat for 6–8 minutes, turning frequently. Transfer the roasting tin to the hob and stir the vermouth and cream into the pan juices. Bring to the boil then season to taste.

Serve with the brochettes and accompany with rice or jacket potatoes and an avocado salad.

GRILLED SARDINES

SERVES

—— 4 ——

For whole sardines, fresh or frozen, grilling or barbecu-ing is undoubtedly the easiest and most successful way of cooking them. Whether you gut them first, or leave them whole, is a matter of personal preference, but either way, use really fresh sardines as they quickly deteriorate in flavour and texture.

Served with some bread and a simple salad, sardines make a thoroughly tasty dish, not quite sufficient for a hearty meal, but unbeatable as a summer barbecue starter.

Gut the sardines if preferred and pat dry on kitchen paper. Score the fish several times on each side. Sprinkle with the salt and tuck the herbs into the cleaned body cavities. (If leaving the fish whole, finely chop the rosemary and thyme and sprinkle over the fish, tucking the bay leaves under and around them.) Leave for 30 minutes.

Shake off the excess salt and grill for 1½ minutes. Turn the fish and cook for a further 1½–2 minutes or until their skins are turning crisp.

TIP

Larger sardines can be gutted and stuffed before grilling. Try the grey mullet stuffing on p. 61 and allow a slightly longer cooking time.

INGREDIENTS

PREPARATION TIME
8 minutes (plus 30 minutes salting time)
COOKING TIME
4–5 minutes

450 g (1 lb) sardines
2 tablespoons coarse sea salt
A few sprigs of fresh herbs, e.g. rosemary, thyme, bay leaves

MEDITERRANEAN GRILLED SWORDFISH

SERVES

— 4 —

PREPARATION TIME
5 minutes
COOKING TIME
6–8 minutes

700 g (1½ lb) swordfish steaks, skinned and boned
2 cloves garlic, peeled and crushed
4 tablespoons olive oil
2 tablespoons tomato purée
1 teaspoon fresh chopped thyme
½ teaspoon white wine vinegar
Salt and freshly ground black pepper

When grilling cubed pieces of swordfish you can rest assured that, unlike many other types of fish, it won't fall apart during the process. Shark has similar qualities and can easily be substituted in this recipe.

If you've time, prepare the fish and steep it in the garlicky, tomato marinade well in advance, so that the flavours mingle. I can recommend the 'sun-dried' variety of tomato purée for this recipe, although ordinary purée will work successfully. To continue the Mediterranean flavour accompany the fish with a selection of grilled vegetables. Simply cut up courgettes, aubergines and two or three types of pepper into manageable strips or slices and brush with olive oil. Tuck them around the fish and grill until just beginning to sear.

Cut the fish into chunks.

Mix the garlic with the oil, tomato purée, thyme, vinegar and seasoning. Spoon over the fish and turn the fish until evenly coated.

Arrange the fish on a foil-covered grill rack and cook under a moderate grill for 3–4 minutes. Turn the pieces of fish over and cook for a further 3–4 minutes until cooked through, basting with any remaining marinade.

GRILLED SOLE
WITH TANGY CHEESE

S E R V E S
— 4 —

A good dish for when you're really hungry, but also rather tired. Use plaice, cod or haddock if it's easier to get and don't bother skinning the fish – the skin is hidden under the rich topping, and helps hold the fragile cooked fillets together.

Line the grill rack with foil and grease lightly. Lay the fillets over the foil, skin sides down.

Mix together the mustard, cream, cheese, herbs and seasoning and spoon over the fish. Sprinkle with the breadcrumbs and cook under a low grill for 6–7 minutes until the breadcrumbs are golden, watching closely and lightly forking the breadcrumbs if they start to overbrown.

Serve with crusty bread and a tomato salad.

INGREDIENTS

PREPARATION TIME
3 minutes
COOKING TIME
6–7 minutes

*8 lemon sole fillets
1 tablespoon grainy
mustard
4 tablespoons double cream
75 g (3 oz) Cheddar or
Gruyère cheese, grated
4 teaspoons chopped fresh
parsley or coriander
Salt and freshly ground
black pepper
50 g (2 oz) breadcrumbs*

GRILLED FISH WITH ORIENTAL BARBECUE GLAZE

SERVES

— 4 —

The occasion will determine the type of fish you choose for this dish. Filleted plaice, haddock or cod make an easy mid-week supper dish, although you could be more adventurous with whole mullet, trout or snapper, or small pieces of salmon, shark or swordfish.

The glaze is also good with barbecued fish. Brush it over towards the end of the cooking time so that it doesn't burn over the heat of the coals.

Cut the fish into 4 portions.

Mix together the ingredients for the glaze in a small saucepan. Bring to the boil and cook for 1 minute.

Lay the fish on a foil-covered grill rack and brush with a little of the glaze. Cook under a moderate grill for 2–4 minutes. Turn the fish over and brush generously with more glaze. Cook for a further 2–4 minutes.

Serve with rice and a pepper salad.

INGREDIENTS

PREPARATION TIME
3 minutes
COOKING TIME
5 minutes

700 g (1½ lb) fish fillets or steaks, skinned and boned

GLAZE
4 cm (1½ in) piece fresh root ginger, peeled and grated
85 ml (3 fl oz) dark soy sauce
½ teaspoon Chinese five spice powder
2 teaspoons white wine vinegar
3 tablespoons caster sugar

SNACKS AND SALADS

Perhaps the worst thing you can do with a fish is overcook it. Consequently it is ideal for light and healthy meals, as nourishing dishes can be put together in mere minutes.

Canned fish features strongly in this chapter. Although there are many to choose from, I've stuck mostly to my favourites, namely anchovies, tuna and sardines, which are equally as versatile as the fresh equivalent. You can throw them into a salad, heat them up or blend them into dips with some highly successful results.

With the ever-increasing range of interesting produce available in the shops, this chapter demonstrates how unusual combinations can form the basis of many delicious dishes.

HOT PEPPERED MACKEREL

SERVES
— 2 —

W hile smoked mackerel fillets served straight from the fridge make a satisfying snack, putting them under the grill first helps to bring out the flavour. It also reduces the oiliness, particularly if you accompany them with a tangy sauce. Use the same method for other smoked fish such as whole or filleted smoked trout, sprats or plain smoked mackerel.

Place the mackerel on the grill rack and sprinkle with the lime or lemon juice. Cook under a moderate grill for 3–4 minutes until heated through.

Beat the lime or lemon rind with the horseradish, mayonnaise, yoghurt and seasoning. Spoon onto plates beside the fish and serve with brown bread and butter.

INGREDIENTS

PREPARATION TIME
3 minutes
COOKING TIME
3–4 minutes

2 peppered mackerel fillets
Grated rind and juice of
$^1/_2$ lime or lemon
2 teaspoons creamed
horseradish
1 tablespoon mayonnaise
2 tablespoons natural
yoghurt
Salt and freshly ground
black pepper

ANCHOVY DAUPHINOIS

SERVES

—— 3-4 ——

Layered and baked, potato 'Dauphinois' is an irresistibly rich and creamy vegetable dish, usually served alongside roast meats. Bury some anchovy fillets between the potato slices and you have a delicious dish that makes a meal in itself. Serve with a refreshing salad to counteract the richness.

Pre-heat the oven to gas mark 4, 180°C (350°F). Lightly butter a shallow ovenproof dish.

Arrange half the potato slices in the dish, seasoning as you layer them up. Cover with half the onion slices and the garlic. Lay the anchovy fillets over the onion. Cover with the remaining onion, then the remaining potatoes.

Mix together the creams and pour over the potatoes. Bake for about 1 hour until turning golden.

INGREDIENTS

PREPARATION TIME
12 minutes
COOKING TIME
1 hour minutes

Butter for greasing
700 g (1¹/₂ lb) potatoes,
peeled and thinly sliced
1 large onion, peeled and
sliced
2 cloves garlic, peeled and
crushed
Salt and freshly ground
black pepper
1 × 50 g (2 oz) can
anchovy fillets, drained
150 ml (5 fl oz) double
cream
150 ml (5 fl oz) single
cream

IMPS ON HORSEBACK

MAKES
—— 24 ——

What you wrap up in bacon as a canapé may say a lot about your character. Use oysters and you're an angel, dried fruits and you're a devil. For the more human amongst us, wrap a smoked oyster together with apricots and prunes for 'imps on horseback' – an appetizer for fallen angels!

INGREDIENTS

PREPARATION TIME
10 minutes
COOKING TIME
4–5 minutes

*8 rindless rashers streaky
bacon
1 × 100 g (4 oz) can
smoked oysters or mussels,
drained
6 stoned apricots, halved
6 stoned prunes, halved*

Stretch the rashers of bacon with the back of a knife. Cut each rasher into three.

Roll an oyster or mussel and piece of dried fruit in each piece of bacon. Arrange on a foil-lined baking sheet and cook under a moderate grill for 4–5 minutes, turning once. Serve warm.

TIP

Choose long rashers of bacon which will still give generous lengths when cut up.

SWEDISH HERRING SALAD

S E R V E S

—— 2 ——

This is a deliciously healthy snack, provided you don't add too much dressing. For a pretty appearance use tiny new potatoes, which can now be bought most of the year. I've used fresh herring, which is easy to get hold of, but to save time you can substitute pickled rollmops, matjes herrings or even canned sardines.

———

Cook the potatoes in boiling salted water for 10–15 minutes until tender. Drain.

Fry the herring fillets in 2 teaspoons of the oil for 1 minute on each side. Cut the fillets into bite-sized pieces.

Mix together the remaining oil, herbs, mustard, sugar, lemon juice and seasoning.

Combine the potatoes, herring and cucumber in a salad bowl. Add the dressing and toss lightly. Serve with crusty bread.

INGREDIENTS

PREPARATION TIME
12 minutes
COOKING TIME
12–17 minutes

350 g (12 oz) small potatoes, scrubbed and halved
3 tablespoons salad oil
2 herring fillets
2 tablespoons chopped fresh dill, parsley, chervil or chives
1¹/₂ teaspoons Dijon mustard
1 teaspoon light brown sugar
1 teaspoon lemon juice
Salt and freshly ground black pepper
¹/₄ cucumber, sliced

PRAWN CHEESE ON TOAST

SERVES
— 2 —

PREPARATION TIME
10 minutes
COOKING TIME
5 minutes

*100 g (4 oz) frozen
prawns, thawed, drained
and chopped
1 clove garlic, peeled and
crushed
75 g (3 oz) soft goat's
cheese, or cream cheese
Salt and freshly ground
black pepper
25 g (1 oz) butter, softened
2 teaspoons chopped fresh
herbs (e.g. tarragon,
chervil, parsley, dill)
¹/₂ small baguette*

This is a really superb snack or light lunch dish that relies on good basic ingredients. Use good-quality frozen prawns. Avoid substituting dried herbs if fresh prove unattainable; instead, stick to parsley and garlic.

Beat together the prawns, garlic and cheese with a little seasoning.

Beat the butter with the herbs and season to taste. Cut the bread diagonally to give 4 long, thin slices. Spread lavishly with the butter mixture and cook under a moderate grill until turning golden around the edges.

Top with scoops of the prawn mixture and return to the grill for 1–2 minutes until warmed through. Serve hot.

TIP

The mini ready-to-bake baguettes are ideal for this recipe and have a better flavour than ordinary French bread. Bake them lightly beforehand.

Store-cupboard calzone

S E R V E S

—— 4 ——

Sardines and another useful standby, a packet of pizza base mix, are here combined in a hearty, fast-food filler. Calzone are simply wrapped pizzas, in which the filling is encased, Cornish pasty-style, in the dough. Like pizza the variations on the filling are endless and can depend largely on what you have in store. Cheese, olives, sweetcorn, mushrooms, spinach and peppers can easily be thrown in. As for the fish, use canned smoked brisling, anchovies or pilchards if you haven't any sardines.

————

Pre-heat the oven to gas mark 7, 220°C (425°F). Lightly grease a baking sheet.

Empty the pizza base mix into a bowl and make up following the packet directions. Knead gently, then cut into four pieces. Roll out each piece on a lightly floured surface to a round, about 18 cm (7 in) in diameter.

Spoon the tomato purée over the centres and top with the sardines. Arrange the cheese, then pimientos, over the fish, and season lightly.

Brush the edges of the dough with the milk then bring up the sides to enclose the filling. Press the edges together to seal and crimp with thumb and forefingers. Brush with milk and bake for 15–20 minutes until golden. Serve hot.

TIP

For a speedier version, make an ordinary base with the pizza base mix and pile the remaining ingredients over the surface, finishing with the cheese.

INGREDIENTS

PREPARATION TIME
20 minutes
COOKING TIME
15–20 minutes

1 × 145 g (5 oz) packet of pizza base mix
4 tablespoons tomato purée
1 × 120 g (4¹/₂ oz) can sardines, drained
150 g (5 oz) Mozzarella cheese, sliced
50 g (2 oz) Cheddar cheese, sliced
1 × 185 g (6¹/₂ oz) can pimientos, drained and sliced
Salt and freshly ground black pepper
Milk for brushing

SMOKED FISH FRITTATA

SERVES
—— 2 ——

These deep omelettes make the perfect dish when you've lots of leftover bits in the fridge. Cooked potato and other vegetables, salami or any delicatessen meats, all mingle perfectly with a little smoked haddock for a warming snack.

Cut the fish into small pieces. Beat together the eggs, herbs and seasoning.

Heat the oil in a medium-sized frying pan. Add the spring onions, courgette, sausage and potatoes and fry gently for 3 minutes, stirring frequently. Add the smoked fish and prawns and cook for a further 1 minute, still stirring.

Pour the egg mixture into the pan and, as it starts to cook around the edges, pull it into the centre with a fork so that the raw mixture flows outwards. When lightly set transfer to a moderate grill and cook for 1–2 minutes until set. Slide out of the pan onto serving plates.

INGREDIENTS

PREPARATION TIME
12 minutes
COOKING TIME
8 minutes

225 g (8 oz) smoked haddock or cod, skinned and boned
4 eggs
2 teaspoons fresh thyme, sage, oregano, marjoram or parsley, chopped
Salt and freshly ground black pepper
2 tablespoons olive oil
1/2 bunch spring onions, trimmed and chopped
1 courgette, trimmed and sliced
50 g (2 oz) salami or chorizo sausage, chopped
110 g (4 oz) cooked potatoes, sliced
50 g (2 oz) frozen prawns

ANCHOVY AND CREAM TOASTS

S E R V E S
— 2 —

This is a good dish to serve for brunch when you don't feel like counting calories. Alternatively serve for lunch or supper with plenty of crisp salad.

Using a biscuit cutter, cut two small rounds from each slice of bread, about 5 cm (2 in) in diameter, to give six circles of bread.

Melt the butter with the oil in a frying pan, and fry the bread on both sides until it turns golden. Transfer the bread onto serving plates and lay the drained anchovy fillets on top. Spoon on the soured cream and season with black pepper.

TIP

Substitute thick Greek yogurt for the cream, if preferred.

INGREDIENTS

PREPARATION TIME
5 minutes
COOKING TIME
2–3 minutes

*3 large, thick slices white
or granary bread
40 g (1½ oz) butter
2 teaspoons olive oil
50 g (2 oz) can anchovy
fillets, drained
150 ml (5 fl oz) soured
cream
Freshly ground black
pepper*

HERRINGS IN WHITE WINE

S E R V E S
— 2 —

This recipe is vaguely similar to soused herrings except that wine is used in place of the vinegar. For a slightly sweeter version use a medium cider.

Tuck any roes back inside the fish. Place the herrings in a frying pan with the wine and water.

Add the onion and celery to the pan with the peppercorns, bay leaves, lemon slices and sugar. Bring almost to the boil, then reduce heat, cover with a lid and simmer very gently for 3 minutes. Turn the fish over and cook for a further 3 minutes.

Serve warm or cold, sprinkled with parsley.

INGREDIENTS

PREPARATION TIME
3 minutes
COOKING TIME
6 minutes

2 herrings, gutted
150 ml (5 fl oz) medium
white wine
150 ml (5 fl oz) water
1 small onion, peeled and
sliced
1 celery stalk, chopped
2 teaspoons black
peppercorns
2 bay leaves
4 lemon slices
1/4 teaspoon caster sugar
Chopped fresh parsley for
garnish

KIPPER TOASTS

SERVES

—— 1 ——

Kippers for breakfast are still a treat for most of us. Sandwiched in a 'French toast'-style fry-up, this hearty snack is both nourishing and satisfying. Try adding a little Dijon mustard or horseradish if you need a kick at the start of the day.

Lightly butter one slice of the bread. Pack the kipper down onto the bread and top with the second bread slice. Cut off the crusts and press the edges of the bread together to seal.

Break the egg into a shallow dish and lightly beat with the milk and a little seasoning. Soak both sides of the kipper sandwich in the egg mixture until all the mixture has been absorbed.

Melt the remaining butter with the oil in a frying-pan. Fry the sandwich gently for 3 minutes. Flip over and cook for a further 3 minutes. Serve hot.

INGREDIENTS

PREPARATION TIME
5 minutes
COOKING TIME
6 minutes

10 g (¹/₂ oz) butter
2 thin slices bread
1 kipper fillet, about 75 g
(3 oz), flaked
1 small egg
1 teaspoon milk
Salt and freshly ground
black pepper
1 teaspoon vegetable oil

BRIOCHES WITH MUSHROOMS AND ANCHOVIES

S E R V E S

—— 4 ——

For this dish you need individual brioches, usually found alongside muffins, pittas and other more unusual breads in the supermarket. The soft spongy centres of brioches can be scooped out to leave pretty cases for all kinds of savoury fillings. This rich mushroom sauce, whipped up with anchovies, makes a delicious filling. If you can't find brioches, spoon the sauce onto thick slices of toast instead.

Pre-heat the oven to gas mark 4, 180°C (350°F).

Slice a 'lid' off the top of each brioche. Using a teaspoon scoop out the centres to leave a case about 0.5 cm ($^1/_4$ in) thick. Place cases and lids on a baking sheet and bake for 5 minutes until turning crisp.

Melt the butter in a saucepan. Fry the mushrooms for 1 minute. Add the anchovies, mustard and cream and heat through gently. Season lightly and spoon into the cases. Top with the lids and serve hot.

INGREDIENTS

PREPARATION TIME
10 minutes
COOKING TIME
8 minutes

4 individual brioches
25 g (1 oz) butter
350 g (12 oz) button mushrooms, sliced
1 × 50 g (2 oz) can anchovy fillets, drained and chopped
1 teaspoon grainy mustard
150 ml (5 fl oz) double cream
Salt and freshly ground black pepper

SPAGHETTI SQUASH WITH BACON AND COCKLES

SERVES
—— 2 - 3 ——

A spaghetti squash is one of the most marvellous vegetables in the way it shreds into fine spaghetti-like threads once cooked. Here it's tossed with cockles and bacon for a healthy and absolutely delicious dish.

Cook the squash in a large pan of boiling water for 20 minutes.

Fry the bacon in a large pan until crisp.

Drain and halve the squash. Scoop out the seeds, then remove the flesh with a spoon and shred it using two forks.

Add to the bacon with the cockles, cream and seasoning and heat through gently.

INGREDIENTS

PREPARATION TIME
8 minutes
COOKING TIME
25 minutes

---

1 spaghetti squash, about
1.4 kg (3 lb)
6 rashers streaky bacon,
rind removed and chopped
175 g (6 oz) cockles,
drained
2 tablespoons double cream
Salt and freshly ground
black pepper

SHREDDED CRAB OMELETTE WITH WATERCRESS AND TOMATO SALAD

SERVES
— 2 —

PREPARATION TIME
10 minutes
COOKING TIME
6 minutes

*175 g (6 oz) cherry or
ordinary tomatoes
100 g (4 oz) broad beans
1 × 170 g (6 oz) can
crabmeat, drained
3 eggs
Salt and freshly ground
black pepper
10 g (¹/₂ oz) butter
1 clove garlic, peeled and
crushed
3 tablespoons olive oil
¹/₂ teaspoon white wine
vinegar
¹/₂ bunch watercress,
chopped*

This is a good, healthy salad with plenty of texture, colour and flavour; it is well worth keeping a can of fish in store to mix with it. The omelette can be served warm or cold.

Cut the tomatoes into wedges or leave whole if using cherry tomatoes.

Cook the broad beans in boiling salted water for 3 minutes; drain.

Beat the crabmeat with the eggs and a little seasoning.

Melt half the butter in a frying-pan and make two thin omelettes out of this mixture. Place one omelette on top of the other and roll up. Using a sharp knife, thinly shred the omelette.

For the dressing, mix the garlic with the oil, vinegar and seasoning. Toss all the remaining ingredients together in a bowl and serve immediately.

*W*HIPPED SARDINE DIP

S E R V E S
—— 6 ——

This light, creamy dip relies on thorough blending in a food processor. It can be beaten in a bowl but will have a thick, paste-like consistency. Serve as a simple starter with vegetable crudités or keep in the fridge as a spread for buttered toast. It will keep for up to three days.

———

Blend the sardines in their sauce, butter and cheese in a food processor until pale and creamy, frequently scraping the mixture away from the sides of the bowl. Season the mixture and turn into a serving dish.

INGREDIENTS

PREPARATION TIME
3 minutes

*2 × 120 g (4¹/₂ oz) cans
sardines in tomato sauce
50 g (2 oz) butter, softened
100 g (4 oz) Mascarpone
or cream cheese
Salt and freshly ground
black pepper*

GRILLED
AVOCADO COCKTAILS

S E R V E S

— 2 —

PREPARATION TIME
5 minutes
COOKING TIME
4–5 minutes

*1 × 100 g (4 oz) can tuna
in brine, drained
4 small gherkins, sliced
2 tablespoons mayonnaise
1 tablespoon single cream,
or ¹/₂ teaspoon top of the
milk
Salt and freshly ground
black pepper
1 large avocado
40 g (1¹/₂ oz) Gruyère or
Emmenthal cheese, grated*

Halved avocados make natural cases for many a delicious filling. Try this tuna and Gruyère filling as a delicious substitute for the more familiar prawns.

Mix the tuna, gherkins, mayonnaise, cream or milk and seasoning.

Halve the avocado and remove the stone. Cut a thin slice from the rounded sides of each half so that they sit level. Spoon the filling into the halves.

Spoon the cheese over the filling. Cook under a moderate grill for 4–5 minutes until warmed through.

GINGERED TUNA AND GRAPE SALAD

SERVES
— 2 —

This delicious salad, assembled in mere minutes, has a tangy, refreshing, fruity dressing, making a welcome change to the more familiar mayonnaise or oil-based ones. Use tuna of your choice – in oil for a moister, richer flavour, in brine or water if you're feeling health-conscious!

Place all the ingredients in a bowl and toss together lightly. Serve with crusty bread.

INGREDIENTS

PREPARATION TIME
7 minutes

1 × 200 g (7 oz) can tuna, drained
1 small red pepper, de-seeded and thinly sliced
2 celery stalks, sliced
225 g (8 oz) seedless white grapes
1 piece stem ginger, finely chopped
1 tablespoon ginger juice from jar
3 tablespoons grape or apple juice
50 g (2 oz) peanuts or cashews

SEAFOOD MENUS

Now that we've diversed from the traditional 'fish' starter and 'meat' main course menu pattern, fish lovers can feel free to enjoy complete seafood meals, whether it's a simple supper or smart dinner party. Here are a few menu ideas taken from the chapters that you might like to try. I've suggested some easy accompaniments to the main course, but leave the choice of dessert open. This might be a simple fruit salad, sorbet or your own tried and tested favourites.

HOT AND SPICY

Indonesian Hotpot   (p. 41)

Seafood Curry   (p. 82)
Basmati rice
Minted cucumber salad

EASY FAMILY MEAL

Smoked Haddock Soup   (p. 20)

Plaice with Chorizo Stuffing   (p. 60)
Spaghetti or penne pasta

COOK AHEAD

Trout Ceviche with Pickled Cucumber   (p. 28)

Tandooried Fish   (p. 49)
Warm naan bread
Mixed salad

SMART
DINNER PARTY

Smoked Salmon and Watercress Soup   (p. 21)

Special Seafood Cocktail   (p. 32)

Whole Baked Fish in Foil   (p. 63)
Minted new Potatoes
Mangetout

CASUAL
SEAFOOD BUFFET

Imps on Horseback   (p. 116)
Smoky Trout Rillettes   (p. 23)
Cod and Saffron Pie   (p. 58)
Oriental Fondue   (p. 73)
Plate of prawns
Warm baguette
Leafy salad

WINTER WARMER

Shrimp Bisque   (p. 18)

Cod and Cockle Pie   (p. 44)

HEARTY BRUNCH

Blini with Smoked Salmon   (p. 26)

Kedgeree with Crushed Spices   (p. 74)

AL FRESCO

Grilled Sardines   (p. 109)

'Quick and Easy' Paella   (p. 79)
Tomato salad
Olive bread

BEAT THE CLOCK

Soured Cream and Prawn Gratins   (p. 25)

Fish and Feta Parcels   (p. 53)
New potatoes
Buttered peas

LIGHT LUNCH
FOR TWO

Gingered Tuna and Grape Salad   (p. 129)

Prawn Cheese on Toast   (p. 118)

SET TO IMPRESS

Salmon Tartare   (p. 22)

Monkfish Brochettes   (p. 108)

Italian Fish Stew   (p. 39)
Rouille   (p. 40)
Crusty bread

ALTERNATIVE
SUNDAY LUNCH

Potted Seafood   (p. 27)

Roast Monkfish   (p. 46) with
Pepper Coulis   (p. 75)
Sautéed potatoes
French beans

INDEX